KEYS AND A MIRROR

Living Your Life with Purpose

JENNIFER THOMAS STEWART

WESTBOW
PRESS®
A DIVISION OF THOMAS NELSON
& ZONDERVAN

WestBow Press books may be ordered through booksellers or by contacting:

WestBow Press
A Division of Thomas Nelson & Zondervan
1663 Liberty Drive
Bloomington, IN 47403
www.westbowpress.com
1 (866) 928-1240

ISBN: 978-1-9736-2160-7 (sc)
ISBN: 978-1-6642-0244-3 (hc)
ISBN: 978-1-9736-2161-4 (e)

Library of Congress Control Number: 2018902452

Print information available on the last page.

WestBow Press rev. date: 08/13/2020

TO MY MOM, ALBERTA M. MITCHELL (1948–2012)

I am grateful for my mom, and that she was able to see me grow up from a little girl to a lady. My mom taught, encouraged, and helped me. She taught me how to take pride in myself, my work, treat others with respect and kindness, and be the best I can be. She gave me the most important thing, and that was love. And now, I am able to share that same love with my family and those I'm around. She was caring and patient, she not only loved her family but had a special love for her community. She knew what my dreams were, and where I was headed; she believed in me, supported me and sacrificed her time for me. Her words were words of wisdom and kindness. I think she talked about my first book just as much as I did, and she encouraged me to continue to write and complete it. She had confidence in me and told me that I can do anything I put my mind to and that she had faith that I could accomplish what I wanted to. She demonstrated unconditional love, always wore a smile and would lend a hand to the entire world if she could. I will remember all the moments we shared together and always treasure what she placed inside of me.

TO MY DAD, WILLIE THOMAS (1950–2015)

I thank God for my dad and the joy that he brought to my life. He always thought the best of me no matter what. He supported and believed in me. My dad was not only a hard worker, but there was never a dull moment when he was around. He demonstrated how to be happy and laugh no matter the situation. I will cherish every minute we spent together. Remembering all that he taught me.

Contents

Author's Note

God expects us to take care of the things he has placed in our hands. What has God given you? Life, good health, family, friends, finances, ministry, a great career? God has your best interests at heart and wants to get glory out of every part of your life. Through Jesus Christ, you have been given the authority and the keys to live successfully. Your faith and actions make it possible for God to work in your life and live victoriously.

The Bible says that it is impossible to please God without faith. If you want God to meet your needs, you must have faith in his existence and believe that your prayer will be answered. It is not enough for you to believe; you must take the necessary actions to receive what you are believing for and want to accomplish.

God wants us to be strong in him and in the power of his might. Putting on the whole armor, so we are well able to stand against the tricks and deception of Satan during those times when he comes to kill, steal, and destroy. We must be prepared at all times. Even though we face obstacles and hardships throughout our lives, no obstacle is so big that it cannot be conquered.

You're more than a conquer; therefore, whatever your hopes, desires, and dreams are, continue to pursue them. If God has given you a vision, stick to it. Satan will try his best to choke the very life out of you using his tricks and schemes. Look in your spiritual mirror and see all that is in store for you. Allow God to show you your gifts, talents, and abilities. Let him establish your plans, dreams, and visions.

Our love for God motivates us to seek and learn of him. It inspires us to gain wisdom and understanding, and discover his perfect will. God wants a personal relationship with us, and he is all we need. When we live a life that is pleasing to him, we will find favor and good understanding in the sight of God and humankind (Proverbs 3:4). When we find God, we find life and obtain favor from him (Proverbs 8:35). God is our rewarder; he will make our way prosperous and show us how to live a fruitful life.

When going through difficult seasons, you must know that breakthrough is near. When you think you can't continue any longer and feel like you want to give up, *don't give up!* God will give you direction through the Holy Spirit, along with wisdom, knowledge, strength, perseverance, patience, hope, and peace to continue. Finish what he has started in you. No matter what the situation, he is right there with you every step of the way, even when things seem unbearable.

You have the power to overcome any obstacle you face, whether it is problems with your family, finances, marriage, addictions, health issues, or anything else. Remember—God has put his Spirit in you!

Acknowledgments

I thank God, my Father and Creator, for giving me his Spirit, which gives me purpose to do great things in my lifetime and in the lives of his people. I thank God for allowing *Keys and a Mirror* to be part of his plan for my life. I am grateful for the opportunity to be a blessing. This book has come a long way, having been many years in the making. Its journey has had many prophecies.

I am truly blessed to have such a beautiful family. My love and appreciation to my husband Kevin Sr. and our children Kevin Jr., Jaleel, and Akhari – I cannot express how thankful I am for your support and encouragement. I thank God for each of you, and I am so grateful for the joy we share, for your having given me the love and encouragement that I needed, and for the constant reminder to never give up on my dreams – You are a blessing to me and I Love You. My heartfelt love and gratitude to Juanita Stewart for all your love and dedication – all of what my mom gave to me; and through you I am reminded of her each day. Thanks for helping with the kids, for all the delicious meals and your conversation, thank you so much. Special love and appreciation to Beatrice Smith; and to my sister Sabrina Sylve, for the special bond we share. Finally, to all who have been a part of my journey in some significant way I truly thank you. Thanks to all my family, friends and colleagues, those of you who have stood by my side through both good and rough times, who have helped along the way, and prayed for me and my family – my heart is overjoyed. May God bless you and your family for being a blessing; it will not be forgotten.

I pray Keys and a Mirror will be life-changing. *Be Blessed!*

Purpose

Isaiah 61 (NLT)
The Spirit of the Sovereign Lord is upon me,
for the Lord has anointed me
to bring good news to the poor.
He has sent me to comfort the brokenhearted
and to proclaim that captives will be released
and prisoners will be freed.
He has sent me to tell those who mourn
that the time of the Lord's favor has come,
and with it, the day of God's anger against their enemies.
To all who mourn in Israel,
he will give a crown of beauty for ashes,
a joyous blessing instead of mourning,
festive praise instead of despair.
In their righteousness, they will be like great oaks
that the Lord has planted for his own glory.

They will rebuild the ancient ruins,
repairing cities destroyed long ago.
They will revive them,
though they have been deserted for many generations.
Foreigners will be your servants.
They will feed your flocks
and plow your fields
and tend your vineyards.
You will be called priests of the Lord,
ministers of our God.
You will feed on the treasures of the nations
and boast in their riches.
Instead of shame and dishonor,
you will enjoy a double share of honor.
You will possess a double portion of prosperity in your land,
and everlasting joy will be yours.

"For I, the Lord, love justice.
I hate robbery and wrongdoing.
I will faithfully reward my people for their suffering
and make an everlasting covenant with them.
Their descendants will be recognized
and honored among the nations.
Everyone will realize that they are a people
the Lord has blessed."

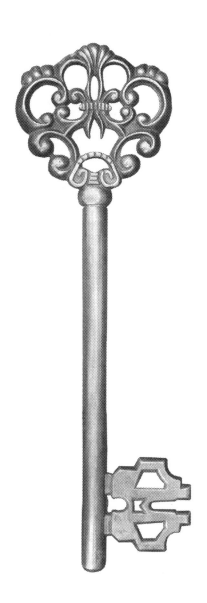

<u>The Key</u>

When you hold a key in your hand, that means you have access to whatever that key was made for. You have all sorts of keys, for your house, car, workplace, and mailbox. The key that you open your car door with is the same key that starts the engine. The key to the car gives you access to go where you want and allow you to lock the door when you are finished. When you are on your job and your manager gives you a key, he or she is giving you the authority or the right to access whatever that key will open or close.

In scripture, a key symbolizes authority. In Isaiah 22:22, we see where a trusted servant received the key of the house of David and wore it on his shoulders. He was given the authority to open and close the door to the king's house. Revelation 3:7 speaks of Jesus having the key of David. It is only through Jesus, by his authority, that anyone can be saved and enter into the kingdom of God. When Peter replied to Jesus in Matthew 16:16-19, acknowledging him as the Messiah, the Son of the living God, Jesus's reply was, "On this rock I will build my church and the gates of hell shall not prevail against it." He told Peter that he would give him the keys of the kingdom of heaven, and whatsoever he shall bind on earth shall be bound in heaven: and whatsoever he shall loose on earth shall be loosed in heaven. In Mathew 18:18, the same was said to all the apostles. In Matthew 28:18–19, Jesus told his disciples that all power was given to him in heaven and earth. And then he commanded them to go forth and teach all nations, baptizing them in the name of the Father, and the Son, and the Holy Ghost. In John 14:13–17, Jesus says that if we believe in him and the works that he did, greater works we will do, because he went to the Father. Whatever we ask in his name, he will do it, so that the Father may be glorified in the Son. We are to keep his commandments if we love him. God has sent us a comforter, the Holy Spirit, the Spirit of truth, that will abide with us and dwell in us forever. The Holy Spirit is God living on the inside of us. We have the Keys.

The Mirror

A daily routine is to look at ourselves in the mirror, to comb our hair and make sure it is not out of place, to check whether our outfit is intact, and to make sure our face looks good. We look in the mirror several times a day to make sure there are no flaws, or we look at what needs to be changed so that the outer appearance is appealing.

When a manager is given verbal authority to oversee the office, he is then handed the keys and has the authority to operate freely, to enter and exit as he pleases within company guidelines. When that manager looks in the mirror, he sees himself as the manager because he has been given verbal authority and the keys to operate in that capacity. When others see the manager, they recognize that he is in authority because of how he operates the office.

When you look in the mirror, you see a reflection of your outer appearance, but if you look closely you can see a spiritual reflection of what you look like on the inside: your attitude, feelings, viewpoints, and so forth. When you look closely at an optical illusion drawing, staring into it, you see a different picture from the one you saw when you first took a look at the drawing. But if you don't ever focus on the picture, you will never see what is going on inside it.

> "For if anyone is a hearer of the word and not a doer, he is like a man observing his natural face in a mirror; for he observes himself, goes away, and immediately forgets what kind of man he was. But he who looks into the perfect law of liberty and continues *in it,* and is not a forgetful hearer but a doer of the work, this one will be blessed in what he does." (James 1:23-25 NKJV)

It is only when we look deep inside our heart and see who we are at that moment that we are able to see what we're created to be, not just staying in one place but growing to a level of maturity and purpose by seeing ourselves as God sees us, which means getting rid of the imperfections and rising to our purpose. The mirror, which represents our spiritual mirror, helps us identify who we really are in Christ. It identifies our current condition and it shows who we are through God's eyes. As with the manager, the Word of God gives us verbal authority, along with the keys, to operate in the kingdom of God. Through Christ Jesus, we have been given the keys to access healing, prosperity, long life, a fulfilling marriage, good friendships, peace, joy, and so much more. Authority is given to those who not only believe in Christ but also are trustworthy and faithful. Jesus said if we believe in him and follow his commands, he will do what we ask of him. When you look into your mirror you should look good on the inside and on the outside.

Be victorious in every area of your life by using the keys that God has given you—and look good doing it.

1

UNLOCKING THE INNER YOU

For many it takes years or maybe a lifetime to find out who they really are and what their purpose is in life. Unlocking the inner you (the real you) is a great journey of faith, courage, trials, and decisions. You find the courage to go through life with its many adversities and its pain. You sometimes go through life making decisions that you think are best, but are not always the right choices. You may not always use the courage needed to go forward, or the faith to walk out of unhealthy circumstances. The inner you (the real you) is unlocked by knowing who you are through the eyes of God. The Word of God defines you. It shows your self-worth and gives you the stamp of approval. When you read and meditate on the Word of God, you see your potential, know your life's purpose, and understand true happiness and contentment. Some agree that money, fame, and earthly possessions identify who you are and what you stand for; but that is only a false indication of the real you. In this instance, the *real you* would embrace your wealth and success and would not allow it to become toxic or detrimental to your life. The real you would desire to live a fruitful life with all that God has given you, looking beyond the material things and titles, making each day for you and others better than the day before.

"But seek first his kingdom and his righteousness, and all these things will be given to you as well" (Matthew 6:33 NIV).

As I was driving one day, the Lord began to show me how I lived my life at that present moment. I went to church, was saved and filled with the Holy Spirit, knew the Word and confessed it over my life, and had love for my family and others. He showed me what was manifesting by my actions every now and then, which did not produce good fruit. God showed me that I was a person with insecurities, unforgiveness, and low self-esteem, and that quite often I didn't know when to shut up. I didn't see myself that way because in my mind I had reasons, or should I say excuses. But given that God knows our hearts, he knew mine. Even if I behaved in those ways once or twice a year, there was no excuse for that. One day of disruptive behavior can change the course of your life, destroy your family, break up friendships, and serve as a stumbling block for someone else, not to mention cause a setback in your own life. One day of selfishness, insecurities, or low self-esteem can cause a lifetime of pain, if you don't know how to identify yourself at that very moment and know who you are in Christ Jesus. During those times of discouragement, I learned to be consistent in my faith walk, knowing that God would do more than I ever imagined.

When you take your eyes off God, you take your eyes off what he has promised, and then things like insecurities, lack of confidence, and low self-esteem show up, which can stop you from moving forward. These are negative personality traits, things that start in the mind and then become visible on the outside. So then you have to ask yourself, *Did my attitude cause a setback? Did I offend someone without realizing it?* Because I focused on what I did not obtain or how I felt my life should be at the time, my attitude could have killed my dreams and altered my destiny. Whether I complained every three months or once a year, it still made a difference. Instead of complaining, demonstrate faith and thankfulness.

God wants us to be in right standing with him. He wants us to live a holy life, a life that is pleasing to him, not sometimes but at all times. Do you know that God is never finished with us? There is always something to learn or work on so that we can be perfected. Each season of our life brings new challenges. It is up to us to know the Word, learn from past mistakes, and work on being better at who we are and what we do.

Minor issues and minor imperfections can turn into big issues and big imperfections that can alter the course of our lives. When we live for Christ, we should produce good fruit no matter what's going on around us. The Holy Spirit wants to direct us and teach us how to live the life God has intended.

When you look in a mirror, you see your facial features. You check to make sure your face is clean and your hair is combed. We should look in the mirror to see not only how we look on the outside but also how we look on the inside. Are you as beautiful on the inside as you are on the outside?

> Just a Thought
> Have you ever seen an apple tree with a few oranges spread throughout? That apple tree should only produce apples, no matter what.

You must be consistent in your walk with God. You, and those around you, should see the manifestation of good works at all times because you are the light of God. The old you with the old way of thinking and doing things, with the same old attitude that's been there for years, should no longer be a part of you if you want to be fulfilled. Don't get caught up in the way people want you to be. God has made you authentic; you are one of a kind, made in his image.

When I allowed God to show me who I was in Christ Jesus, it changed my life. And that meant that I needed to see myself for who I was in God's eyes, and any junk, negative attitudes, bad thinking, and what others thought of me,—all things that did not profit me—had to be done away with.

A lot of times we get in an area where we feel we are all right and that nothing is wrong with us, thinking that it's other people who have the problem. If this happens to you, and if you ask the Lord to show you what you need to work on and what can be better in your life, he will show you—if you really want to know. There is a purpose for you, so tap into your moment, that season where you can be elevated. Allow God to show you every part of you, both who you are at that present time and whom he has created you to be. Find out who the real person is, the one who's hiding behind the hurt and shame, the insufficiency, the tailored suit, and the expensive handbag.

You are the salt of the earth and the light of the world. Never lose your identity, who you are called to be. If that identity is lost, what good will you be in fulfilling your purpose? It would be rather hard to do because you would not have a clue of what you should be doing or why, why you're needed, or what your self-worth is. You are the light of the world and should never be ashamed to let your light, your good works, shine so that everyone can see. Some may not like your light, but don't hide it; it gives life and glory to God.

You are the salt of the earth. But if the salt loses its saltiness, how can it be made salty again? It is no longer good for anything, except to be thrown out and trampled underfoot. You are the light of the world. A town built on a hill cannot be hidden. Neither do people light a lamp and put it under a bowl. Instead they put it on its stand, and it gives light to everyone in the house. (Matthew 5:13–14 NIV)

It is important for us to stay connected to God at all times so that the issues we face do not contaminate our mind and our thoughts. Be mindful of your surroundings and involvement because these things are critical to your success: the people you hang around, your financial status, your living conditions, what you see and hear, your spouse and children, and people on the job. Never allow anyone or any situation to define who you are or dictate your destiny. Let the Word of God define you. When you know who you are in Christ (seeing yourself the way God sees you), you will be free from hurt, shame, and lack, and will be able to move on to possess the finer things—healing, prosperity, wholeness—to a greater degree because now you realize that God created you for his purpose and glory.

Since we face new challenges and grow in faith daily, our no. 1 priority is making sure our life is producing good fruit. The choices we make, whether good or bad, have consequences.

When we open our hearts to God, we are inviting him in to give us all that we need. When we allow God to deal with us, it creates an atmosphere for him to move in our lives. There is purpose on the inside of us. He wants us to birth something in each new season. He wants to steadily increase us and bring us to new levels, build us up and give us an extraordinary life.

Allow God to do what he wants to do with you. *Real change starts with you!*

> "But ye are a chosen generation, a royal priesthood, an holy nation, a peculiar people; that ye should shew forth the praises of him who hath called you out of darkness into his marvelous light" (1 Peter 2:9 KJV).

You are handpicked, chosen by God. There is no one who can compare to you in God's eyes. You are unique with a purpose.

2

BE A GOOD STEWARD

When you hear the phrase *good steward*, money immediately comes to mind. But being a good steward is not about money alone. Instead, it involves everything that God has placed in your hands. What has God given you? Life, good health, family, friends, wealth? The list goes on. God expects you to take special care of what he gives you.

We should take special care of our relationships, the people we're connected to, our spouse, children, family, friends, and colleagues. Our bodies and appearance should be cared for. Our minds should be guarded. We should watch what we eat, both physically and spiritually, making sure we put in that which is of value.

Don't allow things or people to contaminate your mind, because doing so will stop you from reaching your destiny. Beauty starts from the inside and then works its way to the outer appearance. Set a standard for yourself. You may not have everything you want right now, but use what you have and make it work. You may have to wear the same pants or shirt each week, maybe even twice a week, but it's what's inside that counts. There were two dresses I wore just about every other week to church; one was black and the other brown. Now, I could have gone shopping, but then the things I needed for my household would have been neglected. And since money was tight, I wore what I had and didn't care what others thought. I knew what really mattered, and that is the condition of my heart. I could only know this by having the mind of

Christ, as per Phillippians 2:5 (KJV)—"Let this mind be in you, which was also in Christ Jesus"—so that I would be able to be a good steward over all that had been set before me. I would be able to see the beauty, value, and purpose of everything that had been placed in my hands. I had a vision that was greater than the clothes I wore. I knew that if my heart was right, change in my circumstances would soon follow. I knew that if I were to spend time with God, he would surely guide me. It was not easy, but I realized that I would not be in that place always, and as God expands my territory, I would be able to acquire more. I decided to wear my new dress with a clean heart.

When God expands your territory, what will you do with what you've been given?

Many times we make promises before we get what we desire to have, and then when we get what we hoped for, our story changes. What I've learned over the years is that love, patience, generosity, respect, and admiration starts with me. I had to carry all of those attributes before I could share them with others.

We should not pretend to be kind or respectful outside and then neglect ourselves and our family when we think no one is looking. Being a good steward means to take care of everything we possess.

Being a good steward in your household is vitally important. This stewardship starts in your home and then spreads abroad. If you're not a good steward in your household, how can you take care of God's kingdom? How will you be able to give others the help and support they need if you don't practice caring for your family at home? Your household should also have a financial plan in place, along with objectives and goals, which expands your capacity to provide.

What do you want to see happen? What action steps do you need to take in order to reach your goal? Proverbs 16:3 (KJV) tells us that if we commit our way unto the Lord, our steps will be established. When you include God in your plans, he will direct you and align your will with his will. When God shows you his perfect way, there is no room for error. It is when you go off and do things on your own without adding God to the equation that you put yourself in a position to fail. And yes, it may look like it's a win, but at some point you will see there is a void. Let God put the puzzle together for you. Seek his instructions since he is the one who created the manuscript for your life. God knows exactly what you should be doing because he created you to do it; let him lead the way.

God gives us the power (the ability) to get wealth. Don't think for one moment that you are gaining or prospering on account of your own ability. It is foolish to believe that; it is a lie from your enemy Satan, the devil. Deuteronomy 8:18 says, "But thou shalt remember the Lord thy God: for it is he that giveth thee power to get wealth". This means that we should never forget the Lord, and it is through him that we are able to obtain what we possess.

How many times have you thought that you were ahead, and then started slacking off when it came to going to church and praying? Satan wants you to be boastful, prideful, selfish, and non-resourceful. Satan does not want you to come to the aid of others and bless them through your giving. He will throw as many things as he can possibly throw at you to bombard you, to keep you so busy that you miss every opportunity that God has for you. Satan wants you to miss out and does not want you to be truly blessed by God. We should be building the kingdom of God not tearing it down. Make a positive change in your life and in the lives of others. Giving is not only money; you can give your knowledge, skill, or time, or use your ability to connect others with someone who is able to help them.

Money is a resource and is necessary to help us accomplish our visions. It is our resource to provide for our family by giving them the best life possible, take vacations with family and friends, give our kids the best education, have a beautiful home in a safe environment, and so forth. Along with people working together, it is our gateway to building strong, sustainable communities. But we should never allow wealth and material things such as our home, car, or job title to take us out of our place with God and rob us of our future, because God is our source, not material possessions. There is so much more we can do for ourselves and our communities when we use what we have responsibly.

"That you would walk worthy of God, who has called you
to his kingdom and glory" (1 Thessalonians 2:12 KJV).

Do you know that God has assigned people to your life? Not only your close kin, but also people you may not know right now. Never tear down or break a person's spirit because of what you see or think is not happening for them at that moment. Never tear down a person because you're having a bad day. See people for who God has created them to be. See them for where their potential will take them. And it is easier to do this when you know who you are through God's eyes. Then you are able to see someone else in the same light. Ask God to show you how to handle every circumstance and every person you're connected to or come in contact with, whether family, friend, or coworker. And if you have never experienced poverty or lack, count your blessings. But I believe that if you really look back over your life, you will see that at some point you lacked something, maybe a loved one, a friend, good health, peace within yourself or in your home, or faith in God. Do your best with all that God has given you so that you can have a prosperous and fulfilled life. Let your works be pleasing in the sight of God. Keep your blessings flowing.

When people are in humbling circumstances, we should not mock or gossip about them. We should pray for them, and if we are able to do more than that, we should. They may look down and out today, but they have the potential to be life changers tomorrow. The devil is always working to get us off course, and yes, we are tested and tried on every hand. Things may not always go the way we want them to, but the good news is that everything works out for our good. What God gives us should be shared with others, even if it is just a word of encouragement.

"If a brother or sister be naked, and destitute of daily food, and one of you say unto them, Depart in peace, be ye warmed and filled; notwithstanding ye give them not those things which are needful to the body; what doth it profit? Even so faith, if it hath not works, is dead, being alone" (James 2:15–17 KJV).

"As a man purposeth in his heart let him give; not grudgingly, or of necessity: for God loveth a cheerful giver" (2 Corinthians 9:7 KJV).

God wants us to have more than enough for our family and others.

God wants us to be cheerful givers. We should walk in love, joy, peace, longsuffering, gentleness, goodness, faith, meekness, and temperance. These are all fruits of the Spirit in which we should walk daily" (Galatians 5:22 KJV).

> "If there be among you a poor man of one of thy brethren within any of thy gates in thy land which the Lord thy God giveth thee, thou shalt not harden thine heart, nor shut thine hand from thy poor brother" (Deuteronomy 15:7 KJV).

We should not be idle and should work toward the things we want to accomplish. But we should remember those who need some extra attention. It is our duty according to God's Word to give hope and show compassion, not in a weak way, but in love one for another. We should look beyond the outer appearance, see what people can become, and bring out the best in them. Some may not want help and may never grab hold of their full potential. Some may refuse change. Others want to change but do not know which steps to take to make that possible. For those who do not know the steps to take, we should sow into them by giving them hope, knowledge, resources, or kindness, whatever is in our power to give at that moment. We should pull them out of what they are in or at least plant the seed; God will send others to water what we have sown. Nevertheless in all our doings, we must let God lead us.

This takes me back to a time where there was a certain individual who would repeatedly ask for money from everyone he passed. So one day I gave a few dollars to him. On a different day at a different location, I saw this person again, and as before he asked for money. On this occasion I offered him a job doing yard work so that he could have work and make more money. He agreed and never showed up. When I saw him again and was asked to give money, I refused, because it was apparent that he was not ready for change. I invited him to church; he refused and turned his head. So I've learned that I cannot help everyone, but I will make the effort, even if it's just being kind. If that's what I have at that moment, then I will share it. Helping does not mean getting in people's business or being nosy and pretending to help with other motives. This is not what I am implying. And it does not mean putting ourselves in a harmful or dangerous situation. If we ask God, he will show us just how far to take our stewardship.

> Just a Thought
> We shouldn't have to pray about doing good; we know to do good.

Doing for others is not only fulfilling but also life-changing. There was a lady with two young girls who were ahead of me in the checkout line at the grocery store. When the cashier gave her the total she owed, the lady realized she had come up short. She began to take a few items out of the basket. I asked the cashier how much was needed, and I went ahead and added those items to my groceries. The expression on the faces of the woman and her daughters were both *You don't know us, so why are you helping?* and appreciative all at the same time. Even though what I gave was a very small amount, to this family it appeared that they had just received a million bucks. I did not look at their appearances and let how they looked determine whether I would help them or not. God does not want us to be that way. God loves a cheerful giver and is pleased when we show his love and favor. Ephesians 2:10 says that we are God's workmanship, created in Christ Jesus to do good works, which God prepared in advance for us to do.

Look around you. If you look close enough, you'll see the hurt and neglect that people carry in their hearts. Some settle for it, but it's not the truth of the matter. When you are a light and hope for someone, they will truly see Jesus. I decided long ago that I did not want to be broken in spirit or broke in my pocket, to the point that I would not be able to do for myself and the people around me. I didn't want to live from paycheck to paycheck. There were many days when I lived that way, but my goal was to break free, because I didn't want to stay there. In my hardship I learned to endure. It made me stronger, and I am now a better person. Our hardships are testimonies for others so that they can witness real stories of victory. Some may not believe the Bible, but if they see what you've been through and where God has placed you, they will believe in the power of the living God. You are a written epistle.

Allow God to continue to give you wisdom, knowledge, and understanding so that you can reshape the world. Letting God direct you in your giving allows him to use you as his instrument to get what's needed to his people: money, knowledge, food, water, housing, etc. We should all want to rejoice together; at least that's the way it should be.

Never allow yourself to keep someone down or stop them from achieving. Have a desire to love and care for others, not just a certain group or people of a certain caliber. God loves us all and does not want us to hurt. Be excited about your giving, no matter how big or small. See yourself sowing into God's kingdom. What an honor. Think about the lives that will be reached, all to the glory of God!

> "For God so loved the world, that he gave his only begotten Son, that whosoever believeth in him should not perish, but have everlasting life" (John 3:16 KJV).

What if the Lord says to give it all? The first thing that might cross your mind is, *What will I have if I give it all away?* Giving it all may not mean giving your whole life's savings. It could be an extra car that you have no use for and God tells you to give it to someone who needs one. Maybe you don't have an extra car but you do have a piece of property that could be used for a youth development center or for someone who needs a place to live. Or your neighbor might knock on your door to borrow a cup of sugar, even though you only have one cup left until you make a grocery run again.

There are times when God instructs us to give our last so that he can give us greater. In such cases, our faith is tested and our obedience is tried. What we have comes from God anyway, and we must have faith in him, knowing that he loves a cheerful giver and that he will return to us double what we have given to someone else. The person who received can learn how to love again. Or, it may be a lesson for you, where God wants to teach you about yourself and show what he can do through you. This is where real prosperity begins.

In Genesis 22, God tested Abraham's love for him by telling him to offer his son Isaac, whom Abraham loved dearly, as a sacrifice. Abraham followed God's command and built an altar for the sacrifice. When

Abraham stretched forth his hand to do as he was commanded, the angel of the Lord called upon Abraham and told him not to lay his hand upon his son, saying that Abraham had proven that he feared and loved God. Because Abraham did not withhold his son and was a faithful man, God vowed to bless him and multiply his seed, saying that his offspring would possess the gate of his enemies and would bless all the nations of the earth, because he had obeyed God's voice. This passage clearly shows us what God wants to do for us if we obey him in all things.

God's Word is true and alive. Use your faith to tap into God's glory which has been passed down to you from many generations. Look at what God has said about you and what you are capable of doing.

God tests your faithfulness and love for him. He wants to do something for you; maybe it has to do with healing, restoration, financial increase, or your children being saved—whatever you are believing for. When God tells you to move, do it without delay. In order to know God's voice, you must spend time with him in prayer and meditating on his Word. Your family is very important, and that part of your life must be in order, but you also have to expand your thoughts beyond yourself and understand the importance of everything that involves your life. What's the purpose of having a lot of money if you also have a hardened heart, marriage problems, or relationship issues?

We should not be so concerned about our own welfare, plans, and agendas that we neglect our family, friends, and community. Sometimes we have to go beyond giving to charities, churches, and other organizations, because there are many people who do not go to church or receive from charities. What about the guy you see walking to work every day, or that mother who has four kids and can barely make ends meet? They may not meet the criteria charities set for whom they give assistance to, or perhaps they can't find a job or a better paying job. How can you reach out to a person in this type of situation?

What God gives you is not just for you; he wants you not only to support your family but also to be a blessing.

Let God get the glory from your life. That's why it is so important for you to read God Word's, so that you know his ways, how to handle every situation, and what he expects of you. When you do a good deed for someone, that person will remember what you did and eventually will show kindness to another, and another, and so on. People will begin to experience change, and you will begin to see the change. Do not be disappointed in those who don't seem to appreciate what you did for them, because at some point in their life they will remember.

When I would hear people say, "God does not need you because he's God all by himself," I questioned this statement. As I questioned the statement, I thought, *If God does not need me, then why did he create me in the first place, why do I exist?* As it says in Matthew 22:14 (KJV) "For many are called, but few are chosen." God created both male and female in his own image. Throughout my life people have helped me, and I have helped others as well.

God uses us to get the job done. He not only loves and adores us but also wants us to show forth his glory with a willing heart. But, it's according to our will whether we will do the work or not, to be used as a vessel or channel for God to move through. Obedience is what it really boils down to. God has called us to do amazing things, but are we willing to do the work? God's Word will not return to him void, so what he promised has to be fulfilled, whether through you or someone else.

If you are not willing to take on the assignment, then someone else will be assigned. Make sure it's your assignment before you do something, though. Be prayerful in all things, because you could take on something that's not yours to take. That's why it is important to hear from God. There have been times when I have wanted to help someone but God said, "No, it is not time." When God is working in someone's life, let him work. Don't move too quickly or too slowly. Your timing has to be just right. But in everything, be that vessel that is always ready and willing to be used by God when called upon.

> "So shall my word be that goeth forth out of my mouth: it shall not return unto me void, but it shall accomplish that which I please, and it shall prosper in the thing whereto I sent it" (Isaiah 55:11 KJV).

You should be a good steward with your tithes and offerings. The church, as we have been taught, is a physical building that we go to for Sunday worship and Bible study. Today, know that you are the church;

you are that building, the tabernacle that the Spirit of God dwells in. We should not forsake the assembly – God has a spoken word of deliverance for us. He uses his apostles, pastors, prophets, teachers, evangelists, and other ministers in the body, known as the fivefold ministry, which is the hand of God. We come together in the name of Jesus in unity, in one faith, as a corporate body, to praise and worship our Lord. The church is a covering; it restores. It is a place of healing and saving of souls, and of enrichment, love, and everything that God is. The ministry you attend should be a place where you receive the purest form of God's Word. When you bring your tithes and offerings, a window of blessings will be opened to you; you will be called blessed, and the devil will not destroy what you have. This is the foundation of your giving, the access to sufficiency, helping to sustain you and the people you love. If you don't have anything at all to give as a start, give God your very best.

> "By him therefore let us offer the sacrifice of praise to God continually, that is, the fruit of our lips giving thanks to his name" (Hebrews 13:15 KJV).

All that we have is from God and for his purpose. We are commanded to bring our tithes and offerings to the church, which is the storehouse. When we don't bring our tithes and offerings, we rob God.

Malachi 3:8–12 (KJV) reads as follows:

> Will a man rob God? Yet ye have robbed me. But ye say, Wherein have we robbed thee? In tithes and offerings. Bring ye all the tithes into the storehouse, that there may be meat in mine house, and prove me now herewith, saith the Lord of hosts, if I will not open you the windows of heaven, and pour you out a blessing, that there shall not be room enough to receive it. And I will rebuke the devourer for your sakes, and he shall not destroy the fruits of your ground; neither shall your vine cast her fruit before the time in the field, saith the Lord of hosts.

And all nations shall call you blessed: for ye shall be a delightsome land, saith the Lord of hosts.

Be the best you can be for yourself, your spouse, children, relatives, friends, and acquaintances. Maybe you want to add something else to this list, but these are just a few of our everyday basic functions.

- *Personal* – This involves your character, and having standards for yourself, as shown in the way you care for yourself, your health, your hygiene, your walk with God, and your personal goals and dreams.

- *Family* – Raising your kids based on godly principles; treating your spouse with admiration, love, and respect; and raising and nurturing your family according to God's principles.

- *Relative/friends and acquaintances* – Show love and respect toward them, helping them in times of need if you are able to. Be true. In other words, don't gossip about them or their families, but love them. Even if they've hurt you in some way, open your heart and forgive them. Have good conversation.

- *Your job* – Whether an employee, or business owner, you should have good character, with integrity, always honest and responsible.

"Walk in wisdom toward them that are without, redeeming the time. Let your speech be always with grace, seasoned with salt, that ye may know how ye ought to answer every man" (Colossians 4:5–6 KJV).

3

DON'T LET ANYONE OR ANYTHING DETER YOU

Throughout life there are many obstacles and hardships, but no obstacle is too big that it cannot be conquered. Whatever your hopes, desires, and dreams are, continue to pursue them. If God has given you a vision, stick to it. Satan will try to choke the very life out of you with his tricks and schemes. Satan will sometimes use the closet person to you to cause disruption, get you off track, and take your focus off your dreams and the things that God has shown and promised you. Ask Jesus to guide you. Get into the presence of God, read and study the Bible, attend a church that teaches the truth, and meditate on God's Word. Hear and know the voice of God by spending time with him and being in his presence. This is how you have a personal relationship with him. Then he is able to speak to you and you are able to hear and speak to him with confidence and assurance.

Don't give up when you are right at the end of the wilderness experience. The wilderness experience is being in a place or a turning point in your life where you have done all you can do and you are standing and waiting for God to manifest what he has promised. This is where your character is built and where your faith in God becomes stronger. It sometimes feels like you are all alone, but be assured that God is with you. This moment is pivotal because you are put in a position where you will stand on God's strength and not your own. When you go through a difficult situation, you must believe that breakthrough is near and recognize it when it appears. When you think you can't go on any longer and you feel like you want to give up, don't give up. God will give you the strength to go another day.

During this wilderness period, we learn how to trust solely in God and how to walk in his presence with patience and love. We learn about ourselves in the raw. God deals with us in our unprocessed lives. When we are broken, he begins to build us up. The Holy Spirit, God's Spirit in us, begins to show us about ourselves, that which we may not know or may not want to know. It is good for us to see and know the truth because the truth sets us free.

When God is building you, let him build. Take the conviction—it is constructive criticism—and make the adjustments.

Have you ever gone to church and the Word that was ministered seemed to be directed only at you and it seemed like everyone knew your business? I remember feeling this way while sitting in church one Sunday during a time when God was dealing with me on many issues. While the message was being preached, I felt like walking out of church because the word as it says in Hebrews 4:12, is alive and powerful, and sharper than any two-edged sword. But, I did not walk out even though I felt like doing so. The same words that I heard, the entire congregation heard, but it seemed as though the message was only for me. It was then that I perceived, God was perfecting me, and if I would have walked out at that moment, I would have missed what God had prepared – victory, peace, joy, liberty, and hope. Then I would have had to start the process of change all over again.

Let's say you want to build something and the instructions show ten steps to take for a finished product. If you miss a step, if you miss a nail, you will have to undo and start over, because otherwise the structure will not be stable or complete. There is a process or a manner that you have to follow. Since every season in your life may not be the same, your faith continues to increase. At each new level, you are able to see God move and do the miraculous. The Holy Spirit, God's Spirit in you, ministers and show you things about your circumstances that can sometimes make you feel convicted or ashamed, but God knows all things and he loves you.

God also uses men and women who are led by his Spirit to minister and see God's prophecy and revelation; it is God working through them to set his people free. The Holy Spirit makes us free when we allow him to occupy every part of us, which means that there is nothing missing, nothing broken.

Never let your circumstances get the best of you. Keep your eyes on the prize, meaning keep your eyes on what needs to be accomplished and fulfilled. Many years may have passed, but keep pushing toward the mark. God is calling you to a higher level. He wants to give you something greater, so continue to push and press, and push and press, until you reach that new level of glory, of greatness, so that God can show the world his hand.

> "Brethren, I count not myself to have apprehended: but this one thing I do, forgetting those things which are behind, and reaching forth unto those things which are before, I press toward the mark for the prize of the high calling of God in Christ Jesus" (Philippians 3:13–14 KJV).

Know what you are up against. Sometimes you want to fight and argue with people or wrestle with the thoughts in your mind, when you are really fighting against the devil, against principalities, powers, rulers of darkness, and spiritual wickedness in high places. Just like God uses people to bring peace to the earth all for his purpose and glory, the devil will use people and things to cause chaos and bring destruction.

> "For we wrestle not against flesh and blood, but against principalities, against powers, against the rulers of the darkness of this world, against spiritual wickedness in high places" (Ephesians 6:12 KJV).

When trials come to steal your joy, keep you in bondage, destroy your family, or cause your mind to be unstable, are all spiritual wickedness sent to you from the devil, to get you off track and to separate you from the love of God. The Bible tells us to resist the devil and he will flee. Since you are more than a conquer, according to Romans 8:37, never let anything separate you from the love of God, which is in Christ Jesus. Do not give the devil a place in any area of your life. He looks for the smallest opening to come in and destroy.

Know when it is God. When your life is shaken or takes a little turn, it is not always the work of the devil. Sometimes it is God who's moving you into the place where he wants you to be, and to you it feels like a disaster has strike. So, if the company you work for closes, know that God is in control and that he is your source. When your course changes for anything, always know that there is something better in store; stay positive even when it does not look like you are going to make it. During your processing, keep your mind focused, and don't allow the devil to come in and change your way of thinking because of what you see. When negative thoughts come to mind, rebuke them and speak the Word of God over your life, and keep pressing. This is why it is important to know your purpose, so that when your course changes, you'll know when and how to shift. And if you are searching to find your purpose, enjoy the process. God's timing is perfect.

> "For this cause we also, since the day we heard it, do not cease to pray for you, and to desire that ye might be filled with the knowledge of his will in all wisdom and spiritual understanding; That ye might walk worthy of the Lord unto all pleasing, being fruitful in every good work, and increasing in the knowledge of God; Strengthened with all might, according to his glorious power, unto all patience and longsuffering with joyfulness" (Colossians 1:9–11 KJV).

BREAKING THROUGH THE WALL

"Breaking through the wall" is a metaphor to describe the hard work, strength, and time it takes to get your breakthrough. The wall represents your circumstances, including the problems, people, and strongholds in your life, setbacks that keep you from moving forward and making progress. The issue could be financial hardship, lack of self-esteem, a weight problem, marriage problems, or something else. Take a moment to identify obstacles in your life. Now I want you to picture in your mind a brick wall along with all the obstacles you've identified. The next step is breaking through the wall so that you can begin to move forward and be productive. Once you are able to penetrate the wall, you see that by making the smallest hole in it, you are able to tear it completely down. Tearing down walls in your life is not always easy, but with God all things are possible to those who believe. In order to tear down those walls, you must trust in God first, because you cannot do anything without him. God will give you direction through his Spirit, and the wisdom, knowledge, strength, and perseverance to continue in the process with patience, hope, and peace.

The bible shows us the significance of fasting and how important it is for our life. I believe that everyone should fast during certain times. It brings discipline, it destroys yokes, release burdens, gives you power and strength to fight your battles, and brings victory.

> But you, when you fast, anoint your head and wash your face, so that you do not appear to men to be fasting, but to your Father who *is* in the secret *place*; and your Father who sees in secret will reward you openly. Matthew 6:17-18 (NKJV)

You can set a time each day, month, or choose a time throughout the year as a time of cleansing for your body, mind, and spirit, to get closer to God, to hear instructions, and to get answers you need. Your fast may not be like another person's, so make sure you consult your physician if required and learn about fasting. Let God show you what is best for you so that you will know when and how to fast. Do not ignore the call. It is a time of sacrifice just as Jesus sacrificed himself for us.

Let's look at a few issues and their possible solutions, as follows, but find a solution for what works best for you.

- Financial problems
  You can begin to search for a job, or a better job with higher pay. Or you can start a business, work extra hours when your supervisor asks, create a budget and follow it, and refrain from spending impulsively.

- Low self-esteem
Remind yourself that you are special to God, that you are smart, that you were made with a purpose, and that you will have good success. You can also write declarations and say them daily.

- Weight problems
Exercise and eat right. Exercise with friends and family. See your doctor if necessary. Speak positively about the goals you want to achieve.

God wants us to finish what he has started in us and not give up. No matter what, he is right there with us every step of the way, even when things seem unbearable.

What has God put in your heart to do? Is it to start your own business, go to school, get rid of insecurities, love more, renew your mind, be wealthy, raise your children according to God's Word, spend time in prayer and meditating on God's Word, cease from addictive behaviors, stop engagement in sexual immorality and perversions, get out of an abusive relationship, stop abusing others, or something else? You can recognize when God is calling for change, because when he is, whatever needs changing keeps tugging at you, exhorting you to make a change for the better. Every good thing comes from God your Father. He does not want you to be broken; he wants you to be whole. The wall will never get knocked down if you're not constantly chipping away at it, which means making the necessary changes, renewing your mind daily, and getting rid of old habits. With consistency, perseverance, practice, and endurance, keep doing what it takes. Don't give up.

Think about cutting down a tree. As an axe strikes the bark of the tree, it chips away until the tree falls completely. The tree will not fall if you hit it once or twice, especially if it's a big tree. If it is a huge tree then you really need to put some muscle into it, and you could be at it for a while. You'll have to put forth effort and time to accomplish the job. The same applies to your life.

For this very reason, God sent his Son Jesus, our Lord and Savior, to sacrifice his life for us. Jesus is not dead; he is alive and lives in us. He sent us a comforter, the Holy Spirit, who dwells in us.

This is great news! Through Jesus Christ, you have been given the power to overcome any obstacle, whether it is family problems, financial, marital, addictions, illness—or anything else that you face. God wants you to be brand new. He wants you to be born again, a new person in Christ. God put his Spirit in you, and that means you are more than a conquer! There are answers and solutions for all of your situations. Nothing is too big for God.

The devil does not want you to tear down the walls in your life. That's why he will use anyone or anything to stop you, even if it's your family, the ones closest to you. He will use people and try to put stumbling blocks in your way to bring to a halt what you have started. Prayer is necessary and God is your strength. You may be tested and tried, and it might feel unbearable, but you can make it through. Just stay consistent, pray without ceasing, let the Holy Spirit lead you, and resist the devil and he will flee. Pray for yourself, your family, and those you are connected to. Let your heart be filled with joy knowing that God will hear and deliver you, because he said he will never leave you or forsake you. You will come through as pure gold. In victory, you will dance and sing to the Lord for his marvelous works.

Fill in the following:

Walls that I will tear down in my life.
- ✓ _____
- ✓ _____
- ✓ _____
- ✓ _____
- ✓ _____

I will tear down these walls by doing the following actions.
- ✓ _____
- ✓ _____
- ✓ _____
- ✓ _____
- ✓ _____

4

GUARD YOUR HEART

Over the years I have learned to guard my heart. Your heart which is your mind, is where everything takes place or should I say takes root. It is very difficult to guard your mind when you do not allow God to take total control of your life. When your heart is not guarded, it can cause you a lifetime of pain and agony. Negative thoughts, bad decisions, could be passed down through generations as a result of what you created beforehand; it could be the result of your children not seeing a sound family structure, and so they go through life thinking that their life and family is meaningless. Be careful not to make the wrong choices when someone offends you and you've done nothing wrong at all; or when someone close to you is hurting and there's no answer for it. We are tested and tried on every hand. Our faith is tested; Satan is there ready to attempt to step in to destroy your life and cause chaos, and unravel what God has started in you. As a result of many disturbances, lives have been shattered. No matter what the issue may be, it can bring destruction to your life if you allow it to. When your heart is broken or there is a very heavy burden and you're weighed down with junk, it can put a halt to your destiny. A troubled heart can cause you to mope around, feeling helpless and hopeless. It can bring disease and illness to your body, make you lose or gain weight in an unhealthy way, destroy relationships, create a dysfunctional environment for your family, and cause many other problems.

"Above all else, guard your heart, for everything you do flows from it." Keep your mouth free of perversity; keep corrupt talk far from your lips. Let your eyes look straight ahead; fix your gaze directly before you. Give careful thought to the paths for your feet and be steadfast in all your ways." (Proverbs 4:23-26 NIV).

This scripture tells us to guard our hearts, because how we respond to our circumstances, our loved ones, and our friends and acquaintances flows from the heart.

How many times have you yelled at your kids or acted inappropriately because you were upset about another issue that caused you to be angry or hurt? Begin to identify when your actions and words are inappropriate, when you have that feeling of behaving in a way that you know you shouldn't. You know when you do something wrong, pride takes your eyes off any wrong you have done and cause you to not take responsibility for it. Don't be so prideful where you cannot see and acknowledge your mistakes. See your mistakes and your actions for what they are, and fix the problem. Maybe you need to apologize to someone, or perhaps you never received an apology; or perchance someone close to you died, and the burden is so heavy that it literally feels like it's cutting through you. When you hold on to past hurts and disappointments, that is a sign that you do not have full confidence in God to fix your heart and the situation. You have to mature in areas of your life even through the most difficult times and seasons because change is constant. When a trash can is consistently being filled with garbage, it overflows. It is nasty—an eyesore—and it stinks.

If you are one of those people who always have a negative word to say about almost everything, get rid of that type of thinking and behavior, and replace it with a more positive way. When you speak words that tear down instead of build up, you will always be unstable. How about these statements: "I want a divorce"; "I always feel bad"; "I don't want to be bothered"; "I hate that person"; "You'll never be anything"; "This old beat-up car, something always goes wrong"; "I hate my job; I'm not getting paid enough." Instead of complaining, do something about the problem. Ask yourself, *How do I fix the issue and be victorious?* All that garbage is bad for your mind and body. Holding hate and unforgiveness is detrimental to the body. It affects you, and it can affect the person on the receiving end if his or her heart is not guarded.

Our words mean something; it carries value. It can bring life or death—and God wants us to choose life. The words we speak out of our mouth have power - it can create or destroy. Can you think of anything that's going on in your life right now or in the past that was shaped and formed by your words or actions? When you guard your heart, it stops bitterness and resentment from taking root. Even mistakes that you make can cause your heart to become hard, and then you might blame others for those mistakes. Take responsibility for your actions; do not blame someone else for your mistakes. Even when it is not your fault, you are still responsible for your actions. Free yourself from unforgiveness, both for yourself and others.

Guard your heart by taking the following steps:

1. Acknowledge your mistake. Be honest with yourself.
2. Repent to God through Jesus Christ and ask him to forgive you. (1 John 1:9) Open your heart to the Lord, let him know you need him and love him, and without him you can do nothing.
3. Ask God to renew your mind in those areas where you make mistakes and to change your way of thinking if it does not line up with his Word and his will for your life. And let his will be your will. Have the mind of Christ.
4. Make an effort to change your situations.

"From the fruit of their lips people are filled with good things, and the work of their hands brings them reward" (Proverbs 12:14 NIV).

Don't let negative words shape your life or your character. Guard your heart from what others say about you. Don't let negative people shape your world or stop you from wanting the best for yourself. People can say and do hurtful things, and usually it's because they have problems and are unhappy and want you to feel the same way; they are not conscious of what they say and who they hurt and are merely acting on their emotions.

"Casting all your care upon him; for he careth for you"
(1 Peter 5:7 KJV).

WEAR YOUR ARMOR

Therefore put on the full armor of God, so that when the day of evil comes, you may be able to stand your ground, and after you have done everything, to stand. Stand firm then, with the belt of truth buckled around your waist, with the breastplate of righteousness in place, and with your feet fitted with the readiness that comes from the gospel of peace. In addition to all this, take up the shield of faith, with which you can extinguish all the flaming arrows of the evil one. Take the helmet of salvation and the sword of the Spirit, which is the word of God. And pray in the Spirit on all occasions with all kinds of prayers and requests. With this in mind, be alert and always keep on praying for all the Lord's people. Ephesians 6:13–18 (NIV)

TRUTH

Always remember the truth - God's Word. The devil's tactic is to paint a false picture of who you are and what your circumstances look like, but know that this picture is contrary to what God says about the matter. You will only know the truth through God's Spirit. The devil is called the father of lies because there is no truth in him. What is the truth of the matter? God has the final say – what does he say about it? Know what the Word says about you. Your life is in Christ Jesus. The truth makes you free.

"But my God shall supply all your need according to his riches in glory by Christ Jesus" (Philippians 4:19 KJV).

"Submit yourselves therefore to God. Resist the devil, and he will flee from you" (James 4:7 KJV).

"The reason the Son of God appeared was to destroy the devil's work" (1 John 3:8 NIV).

RIGHTEOUSNESS

Know that you are the righteousness of God through Christ Jesus. God did not send his only Son Jesus to condemn us but to save us. We are righteous by faith in Jesus. This doesn't mean that God is finished teaching us or that we no longer need him to work on us. Instead, it gives us the confidence that God will never leave us or forsake us. We are his children no matter what sins we have committed. When you go to God with a sincere heart, he will forgive you and put you on the right track so that you are in right standing with him. Don't let Satan make you feel condemned, as though God will never forgive you. Get yourself back in right standing with God and live your life under his guidance. John 8:44 (KJV) says that Satan is the father of lies and there is no truth in him. Stand on the Word in righteousness.

> "For he hath made him to be sin for us, who knew no sin; that we might be made the righteousness of God in him" (2 Corinthians 5:21 KJV).

> "If we confess our sins, He is faithful and just to forgive us our sins and to cleanse us from all unrighteousness" (1 John 1:9 KJV).

> "And be found in him, not having mine own righteousness, which is of the law, but that which is through the faith of Christ, the righteousness which is of God by faith" (Philippians 3:9 KJV).

YOUR FEET

Your feet are fitted with the readiness that comes from the gospel of peace. We should be ready at all times, walking in the peace of the gospel of Jesus Christ, which has been given to us. We walk in peace throughout our journey. We carry this peace with us, and we bring it everywhere we go. The gospel brings peace. As we walk, we should experience God's peace as it is upon us. Your presence changes the atmosphere wherever you go when your feet are fitted with the readiness that comes from what only God can give you, his Word. You can walk all over the universe with this peace, changing the course of life for everyone, bringing victory to nations.

FAITH

> "No weapon that is formed against thee shall prosper; and every tongue that shall rise against thee in judgment thou shalt condemn. This is the heritage of the servants of the Lord, and their righteousness is of me, saith the Lord" (Isaiah 54:17 KJV).

> "We are made right with God by placing our faith in Jesus Christ. And this is true for everyone who believes, no matter who we are" (Romans 3:22 NLT).

Faith is your shield. Faith empowers you to go into the enemy's camp and take back what he has stolen from you. When firefighters or police officers go into potentially dangerous territory, they routinely carry special equipment including shields to block them from being wounded or destroyed. Your faith works just like that. Faith comes by hearing, and hearing by the Word of God. Having faith in God brings change to your situation, no matter what it looks like, no matter what is thrown at you. You are rooted and grounded, not shaken by what you see, because you know change is on the way. You can keep walking and keep standing because your faith in God shields and protects you. So whatever is thrown at you is knocked down, is put out. Stay consistent.

SALVATION

Salvation can only come through Jesus Christ. It is a gift from God. Jesus said in John 14:6, "I am the way, the truth, and the life: no man cometh unto the Father, but by me" (KJV). When we give our lives to God, we are giving our lives to Christ Jesus for the remission of our sins. Jesus is our entry to God. The Father (God), the Son (Jesus), and the Holy Spirit (our comforter, sent by God to live in us while we are on the earth) are one.

God sent his only begotten son Jesus, who died for our sins and who was resurrected from the dead. God did this for us to give us power to defeat the devil. Because of this resurrected life, we are dead to sin and can live victoriously. When we give our life to Christ, we are born again and made brand new. Jesus said in John 14:12, "Verily, verily, I say unto you, He that believeth on me, the works that I do shall he do also; and greater works than these shall he do; because I go unto my Father" (KJV). All the works and miracles that Christ did while he was here on earth, you are able to do while you live on this earth—and much more.

> "For by grace are ye saved through faith; and that not of yourselves: it is the gift of God: Not of works, lest any man should boast" (Ephesians 2:8–9 KJV).

> "Who hath saved us, and called us with an holy calling, not according to our works, but according to his own purpose and grace, which was given us in Christ Jesus before the world began" (2 Timothy 1:9 KJV).

> "He saved us, not because of the righteous things we had done, but because of his mercy. He washed away our sins, giving us a new birth and new life through the Holy Spirit" (Titus 3:5 NLT).

> "For God so loved the world, that he gave his only begotten Son, that whosoever believeth in him should not perish, but have everlasting life" (John 3:16 KJV).

THE SWORD OF THE SPIRIT

A sword is "a weapon with a long blade for cutting or thrusting that is often used as a symbol of honor or authority."[1] The Spirit of God (the Word) is like a sword; it goes in and it sets the atmosphere. The Word that was given to you in the beginning gives you the authority to conquer

---

[1] *Meriam-Webster Dictionary* (), s.v. "sword."

and be victorious. Whatever the devil throws at you can be cut with the Word of God. Your authority comes from God, through Jesus Christ; this is where you get your right to overcome. God has given you the authority to be saved, to receive healing, to be wealthy, and to be successful. When you study the Word, you learn your rights and you are able to go in and cut down, destroy, open, close, loose, declare, and exalt anything and everything that concerns you, your family, and those around you.

> "In the beginning was the Word, and the Word was with God, and the Word was God" (John 1:1 KJV).

> "Study to shew thyself approved unto God, a workman that needeth not to be ashamed, rightly dividing the word of truth" (2 Timothy 2:15 KJV).

In everything we do, we have to know what the Word of God says about it. We cannot wear part of the armor, but we have to put on the full armor. In wearing the full armor, salvation cannot stand alone. It's not enough just to be baptized and saved in Jesus's name. We can't confess we're saved and believe in Christ Jesus if we don't live our life like him. We still have to follow his ordinances. In order for the armor to be effective, we have to be suited up. What do you think would happen if that police officer or firefighter were to go into dangerous territory without a shield, with a cracked helmet, and with no instructions on how to fight fire or resolve crime? Our instruction manual is the Word of God, which gives us instructions for daily living. It is the answer to everything. If you search it, you will find out that the things you thought were mysteries are now open to you.

> "To whom God would make known what is the riches of the glory of this mystery among the Gentiles; which is Christ in you, the hope of glory" (Colossians 1:27 KJV).

God sent us a comforter, the Holy Ghost, also known as the Holy Spirit and the Spirit of truth. Jesus in not here in the physical, but he is alive and here with us in the Spirit. His Spirit lives inside of us and is our comforter who guides us to all truth.

> "And I will ask the Father, and he will give you another advocate to help you and be with you forever—the Spirit of truth. The world cannot accept him, because it neither sees him nor knows him. But you know him, for he lives with you and will be in you. I will not leave you as orphans; I will come to you" (John 14:16-18 NIV).

Let love be without dissimulation. Abhor that which is evil; cleave to that which is good. Be kindly affectioned one to another with brotherly love; in honour preferring one another; Not slothful in business; fervent in spirit; serving the Lord; Rejoicing in hope; patient in tribulation; continuing instant in prayer; Distributing to the necessity of saints; given to hospitality. Bless them which persecute you: bless, and curse not. Rejoice with them that do rejoice, and weep with them that weep. Be of the same mind one toward another. Mind not high things, but condescend to men of low estate. Be not wise in your own conceits. (Romans 12:9–16 KJV)

PRAY THIS PRAYER

From this day forward I will not speak negative about anything that concerns me, my family, or anyone else. I will not hold on to past hurts or anything that will corrupt my way of thinking and separate me from the love of Christ Jesus. According to Ephesians 6, I will wear the full armor of God daily. I will speak words of wisdom. I will speak words that build up and not tear down. The Word of God says to cast all my cares on him because he cares for me. I will trust you Lord with my life and my heart.

5

FAITH AND WORKS

Consistency, perseverance, and practice. There is no getting around the work and effort that comes with living a blessed life. We must engage in some sort of action in order to survive or create what we see, whether it is picking up a spoon to eat or pushing a lawn mower to cut grass. Everything that has purpose takes work. Speaking positively takes work.

There may be days when all you do is murmur and complain, or maybe your day is not going as planned. Those are the times when you have to make yourself speak positive words and get in the routine of doing it daily. Let's say you want to start your own business. It's not enough to have faith that it can be done. Work is necessary to build your business, such as doing research, obtaining licenses, and finding financing. Not to mention if you get turned down for financing the first or second time around. Will you quit and give up on your dreams if that happens? You speak positive about your children, but are you nurturing them and giving them the love and attention they deserve? How about staying away from the wrong crowd, or working a little harder to save money? *Consistency*, *perseverance*, and *practice* is the key. It is not enough for you to only believe, but you have to take action so you can receive what you are believing for. All takes effort on your part.

> Yea, a man may say, Thou hast faith, and I have works:
> shew me thy faith without thy works, and I will shew

thee my faith by my works. Thou believest that there
is one God; thou doest well: the devils also believe, and
tremble. But wilt thou know, O vain man, that faith
without works is dead? Was not Abraham our father
justified by works, when he had offered Isaac his son
upon the altar? Seest thou how faith wrought with his
works, and by works was faith made perfect?

And the scripture was fulfilled which saith,
Abraham believed God, and it was imputed unto him
for righteousness: and he was called the Friend of God.
Ye see then how that by works a man is justified, and not
by faith only.—James 2:18–24 KJV

Faith and works go hand in hand. When you continue in faith and
works, you will see your blessings manifest. You are actually chipping
away at the wall mentioned in the previous chapter. During these times,
God is perfecting you. You are made perfect in his image and his likeness.
God can do whatever he wants whenever he wants. There is a learning
process for everyone. The processing time and how we are processed
varies from person to person, but it is good for us.

"Now faith is the substance of things hoped for, the
evidence of things not seen" (Hebrews 11:1 KJV).

"For I say, through the grace given unto me, to every man
that is among you, not to think of himself more highly
than he ought to think; but to think soberly, according
as God hath dealt to every man the measure of faith"
(Romans 12:3 KJV).

Faith is freely given to us. It is available for our use. Faith means
depending on God to give us the results we want but cannot yet see in
the natural. It's our hope in God that changes our situation. Our faith is
the evidence of things not seen. Our faith will deliver. It is the evidence,
proof, and truth that the unseen will be seen.

Romans 12:3 teaches us that God has given everyone the measure of faith. So we all have a measure of faith, and therefore we have something to work with. When we hear the Word of God, our faith becomes stronger. There are levels of faith, from little faith to great faith. Our faith increases as we continue to read the Word, pray, and spend quality time gaining revelation of his promises.

> "Then said Jesus unto him, Except ye see signs and wonders, ye will not believe" (John 4:48 KJV).

We must put all of our faith in God. Our faith in him should be a commitment that is unconditional.

When you sit in a chair, you have faith that the chair will hold you. What about your coat? When you put it on, do you have faith that it will keep you warm? So what about God? Do you have enough faith to believe he can do more than what a coat or a chair can do for you? The coat and chair are visible, but God is not, because he is Spirit. It is so common to put more trust in things we can see if they look good enough. If the chair looked broken, you would hesitate to sit, and if the coat was torn, you would be uncertain on whether it would keep you warm. But there could be a chance that maybe you wouldn't fall if you sat in the chair carefully, or you might still put on the coat since it has only a small rip.

Because people don't see God, they won't try him. They do not believe that he truly exists or that his promises are true. And some carefully put their trust in God because of unbelief. Don't allow yourself to stay in heartbreaking conditions for years before you truly believe God. Have enough faith in him to do exceeding, abundantly above all you can ever ask or think. You will never see great works if you don't put your faith into action.

> "Now unto him that is able to do exceeding abundantly above all that we ask or think, according to the power that worketh in us" (Ephesians 3:20 KJV).

> "The power that works in us is the Holy Spirit. Christ dwells in our hearts by faith" (Ephesians 3:17 KJV).

> "But without faith it is impossible to please him: for he that cometh to God must believe that he is, and that he is a rewarder of them that diligently seek him" (Hebrews 11:6 KJV).

It is impossible to please God without faith. If you want God to meet your needs, you must have faith. You must have faith that he exists and will answer your prayer. Unlike the chair and coat, faith is believing in something that you cannot physically see at that moment, but you put all your trust in God knowing that he will deliver, even if it takes days, months, or even years. You trust with all your being that God is faithful. Your faith will be tried and tested, but don't give up. Keep standing on the promises of God. Do not be shaken or moved.

God tells us to be strong in him and in the power of his might, so we must put on the whole armor of God—not only the parts we want, but the whole armor. This is how we stand against the wiles (tricks, deception) of Satan during those times when he comes to kill, steal, and destroy us. We must be prepared at *all times* because Satan is always up to something and *it's not for our good*.

During those times when you have done all to stand, you should stand. Do not make excuses for why you are not victorious. God called us to be victorious through Jesus. God has given you the same power to rule and reign and to defeat the devil.

> "The desire of the slothful killeth him; for his hands refuse to labour" (Proverbs 21:25 KJV).

We are all saved by God's grace through our faith in Jesus. You must have faith to know that by God's grace you are saved. When you are saved, it positions you to live a blessed, fulfilled life. Don't get so wrapped up in the same routine, with the same results, no increase, and no change. It is essential to be more than just saved. Being saved not only means that you have salvation but also means a renewing of your mind. There should be changes and adjustments made on your part. Your old ways are to be done away with. There must be a newness that springs forth in your life. This newness, the changes, will bring the results you need to live a prosperous and effective life. You are not the same person you were before allowing Jesus Christ to come into your life to save you. When you make this decision, your life should no longer be the same. You are no longer that old person; you are no longer dead but are *alive* by the blood of Jesus.

Therefore, if anyone is in Christ, he is a new creation; the old has gone, the new has come! All this is from God, who reconciled us to himself through Jesus Christ and gave us the ministry of reconciliation: that God was reconciling the world to himself in Christ, not counting men's sins against them. And he has committed to us the message of reconciliation. We are therefore Christ's ambassadors, as though God were making his appeal through us. We implore you on Christ's behalf: Be reconciled to God. God made him who had no sin to be sin for us, so that in him we might become the righteousness of God. (2 Corinthians 5:17–21 NIV)

> "Jesus said to him, I am the way, the truth, and the life. No one comes to the Father except through Me" (John 14:16 KJV).

> "The Spirit of a man is the lamp of the Lord, searching all the inner depths of his heart" (Proverbs 21:27 NKJV).

The Holy Spirit leads and guides us, teaching us how to discern right and wrong. The way of God is perfect, so let the Holy Spirit have free rein in your life. You will never be misguided, misled, or mistreated. The Holy Spirit will speak to you about your situations and circumstances, and will give you direction and answers. Don't ignore this precious gift that God has given to you. The Holy Spirit is God living inside of you. The Holy Spirit is power and love, everything that God is. You have it inside of you. You're a conqueror.

> "Nay, in all these things we are more than conquerors through him that loved us. For I am persuaded, that neither death, nor life, nor angels, nor principalities, nor powers, nor things present, nor things to come, Nor height, nor depth, nor any other creature, shall be able to

separate us from the love of God, which is in Christ Jesus
our Lord" (Romans 8:37–39 KJV).

Be persuaded, be convinced, that nothing will ever separate you from
the love of God, which is in Christ Jesus. Friends, acquaintances, family,
job, material possessions—let nothing separate you. It is vital that you
stay connected to God through Jesus if you wish to live a successful life.
Problems/issues may arise, but they will all be conquered through Jesus
Christ.

> "But ye shall receive power, after that the Holy Ghost is
> come upon you: and ye shall be witnesses unto me both
> in Jerusalem, and in all Judaea, and in Samaria, and unto
> the uttermost part of the earth. Acts 1:8 (KJV)

The Holy Spirit gives us *power!* This is God working in us. We are
nothing without his power. His power will help us to overcome every
obstacle, every situation, every test, and every trial. If you haven't already,
this day receive God's Spirit, a precious gift that God gave us. We are not
alone; Jesus wants to live inside you and me.

The Bible says that if you ask, it shall be given; if you seek, you shall
find; and if you knock, the door shall be opened. God wants you to find
him, come to him, acknowledge him, and love him. What others say are
the mysteries of God can no longer be hidden from you when you seek
his face, when you have a burning desire to commune with him and be
in his presence. All those things that you thought were hidden will no
longer be, because he will give you wisdom, knowledge, and instruction
for a prosperous life through the Holy Spirit. One important factor is that
you should allow God to move and make changes in your life. That is a
choice. Don't hinder the flow and don't delay the timing. A lack of change
and commitment does not get you very far.

> "But seek ye first the Kingdom of God, and His
> righteousness; and all these things shall be added unto
> you" (Mathew 6:33 KJV).

What changes will you make to seek God (e.g., wake up early, set aside time each day, take fifteen minutes of your lunch break to pray)? Evaluate your day and make the adjustments. You'll be glad you did!

I'm going to make time for God by doing the following:

1. _____
2. _____
3. _____
4. _____
5. _____

You are created in the image of Christ Jesus to do good works, to be fruitful (to do good in the kingdom of God), to help the poor, to love, to share the good news of Christ, to bless the kingdom financially, and to live a holy life. God wants you to walk in perfection.

6

DON'T MISS OUT ON YOUR OPPORTUNITY

Opportunity is defined as "a favorable or suitable occasion or time." It is "a chance for progress or advancement."[2] How many times have you second-guessed yourself, and then when you look back, you regret not taking the opportunity that was presented to you? Again, this shows how important it is to hear from God with confidence.

There are seasons in our life. In these seasons there are doors that will open and doors that will close. Not every opportunity that presents itself is one that should be grabbed ahold of. There are some opportunities that are wrapped up in beautiful packaging with cute little bows, but these could cause a setback and more problems than they are worth. Just like a gift, opportunities come in all wrappings, shapes, and sizes, so to speak. The wrapping may be wrinkled with a small tear at the corner and a ribbon that's raveled, but there is a stunning gift inside the package.

> "Beloved, believe not every spirit, but try the spirits whether they are of God: because many false prophets are gone out into the world" (1 John 4:1 KJV).

Test the things that are presented to you and see if they are of God.

---

[2] *American Heritage Dictionary* (), s.v. "opportunity"

Pray for discernment so that you will know what will profit you and what will hinder you. Be curious to see if God is surprising you with something special. Don't let those opportunities pass you by. When something comes into your life, test it, pray, and inquire. Because God wants to shower you with his love and blessings, he will send something special for you. The reason you should pray about opportunities is that all may not be from God, so you don't want to be blindsided. On the other hand, the Lord could show you your opportunity before it happens. In this case, when the opportunity is presented, you know that it's time to move. When my job ended at the company I was employed with, I did not worry, because I knew beforehand what I needed to do with my time, and that was to focus on previous plans that I had started but had not been able to bring to fruition. So when the time came, I embraced the opportunity, knowing that one door was shut but more doors would be opened. During this time, I began to plan new ventures and complete previous projects. Romans 12:11 (KJV) says that we should not be slothful in business but fervent in spirit, serving the Lord.

Matthew 25 speaks of ten virgins who took their lamps out to meet the bridegroom. The five wise virgins took oil with them for their lamps. The five foolish ones did not take oil with them. While waiting for the bridegroom, they all fell asleep. When it was announced that the bridegroom was there, the five wise ones trimmed their lamps, and the other five panicked because their lamps were going out and they had no oil. While the five foolish ones went out to buy oil, the five wise ones went into the banquet and the door was shut. When the other five returned, they asked to be let in, but the door was kept shut. And they were told to keep watch, as one never knows the day or the hour when the bridegroom will come. So what happened here is that the five foolish missed out on their opportunity because they were not prepared. The door was opened, but because they had not prayerfully prepared for the moment, they did not know what was needed, what they needed to do, how to go about doing it, and so forth. The ending would have been better for them if they would have tested, prayed, and inquired. God wanted to bless them, but because they did not skillfully prepare, they missed out on an opportunity that would have changed their lives. This is why we should always expect and watch for miracles and blessings, because we never know when they will show up. So be prepared, with expectation and confidence, wisdom, knowledge, and understanding, to walk through the doors that have been opened for you.

> "That ye be not slothful, but followers of them who through faith and patience inherit the promises" (Hebrews 6:12 KJV).

Learn to control and train your thoughts. Do not allow your mind and emotions to make you fearful, and don't procrastinate, which can lead you to a path other than the one you should be on. How many times during a day do you say "I'll do it tomorrow," or "I'll do it later on, when I have the time"? Pay close attention to those thoughts. When my children get home from school, I tell them to start their homework. If they do not and starts to do something else like watch TV or draw, when it is time for them to go outside to play, they will not be able to because they procrastinated. So now their homework has to be done during their playtime. It is the same with the human mind. Don't procrastinate, because when something else comes up and is a priority, what you should have worked on prior is still there, staring you in the face. When that door of opportunity presents itself, you are not ready to walk in. With my children, when it was playtime, they were not ready for playtime because they did not prepare for it. So the end result is, disappointment because their homework is not completed and their leisure time was missed. Let's take it a step further – because of this missed opportunity to play and have free time, they could have missed out on meeting new friends, learning new games, riding their bikes, enjoying snacks, all the good stuff. This is just an example of how we can miss out on not only walking through the door but also all the blessings that are on the other side of it.

In Luke 14 (KJV) there is a parable of a certain man who prepared a great banquet and invited many guests. When the man sent out his servant to tell his invited guests that everything was ready, they all made excuses. So the man sent out his servant to gather the poor, crippled, blind, and lame, and all from the roads and country lanes, so that his house could be full. Again, we see a door that was opened and then closed to guests who did not take the opportunity to walk in because of their excuses. A new door was opened to those who were poor, were sick, or were from the streets, alleys, and country roads. These guests took the opportunity and walked through a door that was prepared for them, which I'm sure changed their lives forever.

IF YOU JUST AGREE ....

Missed opportunities can be caused by disagreements. Are you allowing yourself, other people, or other things to cause separation in areas of your life? There is power in agreement and partnership.

> "Now I beseech you, brethren, by the name of our Lord Jesus Christ, that ye all speak the same thing, and that there be no divisions among you; but that ye be perfectly joined together in the same mind and in the same judgment" (1 Corinthians 1:10 KJV).

> "If there be therefore any consolation in Christ, if any comfort of love, if any fellowship of the Spirit, if any bowels and mercies, Fulfil ye my joy, that ye be likeminded, having the same love, being of one accord, of one mind" (Philippians 2:1–2 KJV).

If you want to accomplish anything in life, you have to be perfectly joined together, having the same mind, the same goals, and seeing the same results. This applies to any setting, be it your family, job, business, health, finances, or relationships. The issue of not being joined together plays a role in failed marriages, broken homes, a low sense of self-worth, division in the church, unsuccessful business ventures, and ruined relationships. People are not perfectly joined. Disagreements and jealousy can also cause division. These areas cause you to lose focus and are sources of major damage. Another cause of division is when everyone has their own agenda; no one wants to follow through with the original plan or goals. How many times have you started a project and your sole purpose was to complete it but there were interferences that took it in another direction, and as a result there was no completion and no fulfillment? Don't get me wrong, I'm not saying that everything will go according to plan. And yes, sometimes there will be disagreement. But, the ultimate goal is to finish what you've started and be successful in doing so. With completion and following through, everybody is doing their part, perfectly joined together, with no division, having the same mind. This is a beautiful picture of a fulfilled life. Have the same mind as your spouse. If your spouse sees a new house or a better job in the future, then you should be of the same mind and see the same. If you see your children doing well in school, they should also see themselves doing well. If your child does not see herself doing well, then you should see her doing well, because your thoughts about anything should always be God's thoughts about the matter.

Our mind and thoughts are so powerful, that it can bring the negative back to focus.

> "Let this mind be in you, which was also in Christ Jesus"
> (Philippians 2:5 KJV).

You have to take the appropriate actions to produce what you see. So in this case, you would begin to spend time with your child, letting her know that she is special and what God's Word says about her. Be perfectly joined together. Have the same mind, the mind of Christ.

What's your vision for your job or business? Is it just to say you have a job or business, or is it for a stated purpose? Do you just have employees or contacts so you can say you know people, or do you have them so that they can be utilized for their knowledge, skills, and resources to help produce the best results possible and improve themselves in the process?

What about your family – Do you just have a family with no support and provision? Or, do you see your family as a legacy to help make the world a better place; a place with morals, value, and love.

When we begin to pull in other directions without expression, then we go against the grain; when our objectives change without proper communication. And yes, the reason may be legitimate, and yes, it could be a better solution than the one proposed, but the agreement has been knocked out of joint because of a lack of communication. The opposite party should be given the opportunity to see the matter in a different light and weigh it the same. So when the other party is not aware of changes of focus and does not get the opportunity to speak on that matter, it causes chaos in the camp. Then there is a tug-of-war. One person pulls in one direction, and the other in the other direction, and nothing ever gets accomplished. In the process everything else falls apart, along with the family structure, relationships, career or business. So now something else has come in to play that has taken everyone off course. The ultimate goal is no longer the same. What do you think would happen if you and a hundred other people went on a cruise bound for a certain destination and everyone was in agreement about that destination before leaving? Then when you get far out into the sea, the captain and his crew decide to go in a different direction without informing you of the changes and the reason, but want you to continue to cruise. What would be the reaction of the passengers? People would panic, become emotional, and have words for the captain and words with each other. Some may even want to get off the boat.

Even if no one knows what your plans are but you and God, you still have to be perfectly joined with God having the same mind as he, and perfectly joined with others. Apart from God, whatever you are wanting to accomplish will not work, even if it seems to be, ultimately there will be something missing, and he has the answer for everything that concerns you.

What do you want to accomplish? What has God told you to do – complete college, restore wounded relationships, have good success, live a fruitful life, love others, be committed to your spouse, wait on your spouse, spend time with your family. Are the people around you in agreement with you? Are you in agreement with them? And lastly, what are you agreeing on?

Again, what are you agreeing on? Remember that there is power in your words and thoughts. When thoughts and ideas come your way and they don't agree with God's, you have to quickly rebuke them. Speak to those thoughts, and say what God says about the matter. Your thoughts and words can cause hindrances to others as well as to you, and you don't want to be a part of that. Has anyone ever said anything negative about you repeatedly? Believe it or not, those words can follow you and attach themselves to you if you let them. People have to work harder to rid themselves of negative words spoken. For instance, let's say a person has a nickname like "Angry Man" or "Slowpoke" and that this name was given to him since he was very young, with no one seeming to think anything of it. And sometimes that's the case, people issue nicknames for fun and in their mind it won't cause harm, but that's not always true.

Even though you see a characteristic in a person or situation, be mindful how you label. When a person is nicknamed, many people begin calling that person by that name, which could possibly open a door for this name to manifest itself. Remember—there's power in agreement, whether good or bad. So now you have many people in agreement, calling this person by their nickname, and now this name is attached to them everywhere they go. What could be the outcome for the nickname Slowpoke – walk and talk slow, does everything slow and has done so for years. On the other hand, angry man always gets into trouble because of his anger. Your words are not giving your situation a chance and are not helping others to excel. Negative words and thoughts get into the heart of people if they allow them to do so, and the content of those words becomes the norm for their lives. Get the picture?

Let's take a look at Genesis 11:1–6 (KJV):

> And the whole earth was of one language, and of one speech.
> And it came to pass, as they journeyed from the east, that they found a plain in the land of Shinar; and they dwelt there.
> And they said one to another, Go to, let us make brick, and burn them thoroughly. And they had brick for stone, and slime had they for morter.
> And they said, Go to, let us build us a city and a tower, whose top may reach unto heaven; and let us make us a name, lest we be scattered abroad upon the face of the whole earth.
> And the Lord came down to see the city and the tower, which the children of men builded.
> And the Lord said, Behold, the people is one, and they have all one language; and this they begin to do: and now nothing will be restrained from them, which they have imagined to do.

As you can see, everyone was of the same accord. They had the same goal, to build a city, and a tower that would reach heaven. In verse 6, the Lord said that because the people were in unity, speaking the same, having the same goal, whatever they imagined to do, nothing could be kept from them. The Bible says that we have the choice to choose life or death, blessing or cursing. God wants us to choose life. The Lord commands the blessing when there is unity (Psalm 133 KJV).

> "I call heaven and earth to record this day against you, that I have set before you life and death, blessing and cursing: therefore choose life that both thou and thy seed may live" (Deuteronomy 30:19 KJV).

> "Behold, how good and how pleasant it is for brethren to dwell together in unity! It is like the precious ointment upon the head, that ran down upon the beard, even Aaron's beard: that went down to the skirts of his garments; As the dew of Hermon, and as the dew that descended upon the mountains of Zion: for there the Lord commanded the blessing, even life for evermore" (Psalm 133 KJV).

> "Endeavouring to keep the unity of the Spirit in the bond of peace. There is one body, and one Spirit, even as ye are called in one hope of your calling; One Lord, one faith, one baptism, One God and Father of all, who is above all, and through all, and in you all. But unto every one of us is given grace according to the measure of the gift of Christ" (Ephesians 4:3–7 KJV).

> "If there be therefore any consolation in Christ, if any comfort of love, if any fellowship of the Spirit, if any bowels and mercies, Fulfil ye my joy, that ye be likeminded, having the same love, being of one accord, of one mind" (Philippians 2:1–2 KJV).

Christ was and still is joined together in unity with the Father (they are one), as he has been from the beginning. Read the Word of God and learn of all the excellent works he has done and is still doing today. There was and still is unity between the Father, Son, and Holy Spirit. They are one.

Pride keeps you from being honest with yourself and it keeps you in a place where you fail to tap into good opportunities. Pride is a disadvantage to you and should not be part of your character. What happens when you let go of a yo-yo? It continues in the same motion, up and down, and is never stable. So one day you're up and one day you're down, exercising bad behaviors over and over again. This is what we do to God when we walk in our own way and not God's way. One day you show love, and the next day you walk with a frown; one day you're ready to work, and the next day you're not. The string on the yo-yo stays on the same track, and the yo-yo does the same thing each time you let it go. There will be trying times, but we should learn how to conquer stressful times and to love ourselves and the people around us.

I am going to make the following changes in my life:

1. _____
2. _____
3. _____

7

A SENSE OF URGENCY: THE PRESSURE IS ON

Have you ever wondered why there are setbacks and delays in your life? It can be frustrating at times to want something good to happen for you, but it seems as though nothing is moving in your favor. There are three important things that we should keep in mind when we are at a place in our lives where we feel that we have done all we can do, and we're tired and frustrated about our circumstance – when there is an urgency for change but no response from God: Our vow, timing, and planning; when change is required but it seems as though God is silent.

YOUR VOW

"When you make a vow to God, do not delay in fulfilling it. He has no pleasure in fools; fulfill your vow" (Ecclesiastes 5:4 NIV).

When you make a vow to God, keep it—fulfill it. What vows have you made to God? Have you vowed to be a better spouse, to be a better parent, to treat others fairly, to do away with gossiping, to stop sabotaging the plans of others, or to be a true friend? Do you sometimes say you are going to do better in certain areas and then find yourself not fulfilling all that you said you would do? When you make a vow to God, you are saying, "God, you are in the driver's seat. I want to live a life that is pleasing to you." When you don't obey God, there can be setbacks and delays. When you put a stumbling block before others or cause offense, you are setting yourself back. You are not only hurting the other person, but also yourself. God will not allow you to hurt others and then bless you for it; hurting someone intentionally will cause a setback.

Don't allow God's favor and blessings to be delayed in your life. Renew your vows with God if you haven't done so, and get back in your rightful place with him. Just like husbands and wives renew their vows and recommit themselves to each other, you do the same with God, because you are married to him. When you make a vow, at that moment you know in your heart what you should do. If you've decided to be better at anything, in the process don't continue to treat others unfairly, be selfish, be arrogant, or be easily influenced by negativity; all these things can cause a disturbance and setback. Don't allow yourself to continue to fall into the same situations over and over. When you know better, you are without excuse. Renewing your mind is very important. Not only should you renew your mind, but also you should take action and be consistent in your walk.

Following is a simple prayer to pray. Feel free to add anything else you want to say.

Lord God, I recommit myself to you. Forgive me for not fulfilling the vows that I have made with you. Right now, I am recommitting myself to you and will fulfill those things that you expect of me, so that there will be no setbacks in my life. Your plan is perfect. In Jesus Name, Amen.

THE APPOINTED TIME

"This vision is for a future time. It describes the end, and it will be fulfilled. If it seems slow in coming, wait patiently, for it will surely take place. It will not be delayed" (Habakkuk 2:3 NLT).

Be assured that what God has promised you will come to pass in its season. When it seems as though it will not spring forth or is lingering,

God says to wait for it. Have faith and hold on to what he has promised to do for you and it will not delay itself; there's an appointed time. When I was about twenty-seven years old, I made a road map for myself of the path to all the things that I wanted to accomplish once I reached thirty. But things did not quite work out the way I had planned them. Through the years and in the process, I learned that timing is everything—and my timing was not always perfect. I was sometimes impatient and moved too fast, and sometimes I moved too slow. When I should have been listening or working toward the next step, I decided to do something else. But whatever the case may have been, God was still there. I began to notice God moving people and things around me, moving some people out of my life for a season and connecting me with new people, clearing up situations, and so much more. I am a planner, I have to admit. It is good to have a plan so that you are not just going through life casually with no sense of direction or urgency. During this time, I was frustrated, uncertain, and impatient. When things did not work out as I had planned, I had my own pity party, which did me no good. I could practically taste success. With all of that, there was so much that I needed to learn before God would put me in charge of everything I wanted. So the lessons went on and I learned that I needed to mature. Over the years I thought I had it all together, but I didn't. There was so much more for me to learn.

When I look back, I see that it was all for one reason: purpose. There were times when I procrastinated, doing what I wanted to do instead of what I needed to do. And for years I thought I was ready, but I really wasn't. God's plan and timing is perfect. I learned to give my plans over to God and say, "This is what I have come up with, but Lord, I need you to make it perfect for me." It was then that I began to see myself going from glory to glory, from faith to faith. At some point, I was no longer having my own pity parties. My faith began to increase day by day, and I began to be content in the season I was in. I began to seize those moments, even though at times it was not easy. I slowly began to praise God in the midst of my trials and circumstances. When the heat turned up and situations got harder, my faith turned up. I'd never, ever dreamed that some of the things that I have faced would ever happen, but I had to stay focused. Through it all, God remained faithful. In the process, I was being prepared for something great.

"And not only so, but we glory in tribulations also: knowing that tribulation worketh patience; And patience, experience; and experience, hope: And hope maketh not ashamed; because the love of God is shed abroad in our hearts by the Holy Ghost which is given unto us" (Romans 5:3–5 KJV).

INCLUDE GOD IN YOUR PLANS

"Commit to the Lord whatever you do, and he will establish your plans" (Proverbs 16:3 NIV).

Our daily activities can be very consuming, especially if there are others who require our time and attention. Sometimes it seems as though there are not enough hours in a day to complete everything that needs to be done. We make our to-do lists and weekly schedules, and sometimes take it a step further, by making a monthly agenda. Getting caught up in the scheme of things makes it easy to forget to include God in the planning process.

Make a conscious effort to let him lead you in your planning stages. This can be added in your prayer or during your planning time, or you may realize it during the tasks. Whether what you are dealing with is personal or related to family, friendships, or work, the Lord will show you exactly what to do, where to go, whom to speak with, what to say, and how to say it. This will help you make better choices in the long run and cause less havoc in your daily routines.

"For I am ready to set things right, not in the distant future, but right now! I am ready to save Jerusalem and show my glory to Israel" (Isaiah 46:13 NIV).

God gives us the assurance that he is working everything out for our good. He tells us that he's ready to bless right now. He is ready to save his people and show his glory through us. We are blessed daily with food, shelter, clothing, good health, a job, family, friends, and anything else that's good and wholesome for our lives. Never undervalue God's power or his love for you.

REFLECTION

The meteorologist gave a weather forecast stating that a cool front would be coming in to our area. During the middle of the night, I woke up hearing strong wind, heavy rain, roaring thunder, and lightning. After the storm was over, the cool front was ushered in. Days before the storm it was very hot and humid. Just like our lives, when breakthrough is near we may begin to experience chaos. All kinds of issues may appear that can sometimes take our attention from our victory.

It may seem rough for a while, but the season will come when you will see and feel a calming and refreshing coolness from the storm, a sign of relief that takes you to a new level. The closer you get to your breakthrough, the more frequent and harder to endure the storms (finances, negative people, broken families, turmoil, etc.) become. Whenever a storm comes, successful people deal with the difficult situation and weather it. If you do the same, it will increase your faith, make you stronger, bring you closer to your purpose, and give you a testimony to help someone else.

8

CLOTHE YOURSELF IN RIGHTEOUSNESS

> "God has united you with Christ Jesus. For our benefit God made him to be wisdom itself. Christ made us right with God; he made us pure and holy, and he freed us from sin" (1 Corinthians 1:30 NLT).

How do you see yourself? Are you giving yourself the credibility you deserve?

Scripture tells us that we are one with God through Jesus Christ. Because we are one with God, our life is untainted, made whole, blessed, holy, and free from sin. No matter what we have done, if we quickly repent with a sincere heart and move away from sin, we are able to get back in our rightful place with God, which is what he planned for us from the very beginning. Before we came into this world our life was predestined. It was already orchestrated. God knew everything about us. Jesus came so that we might have life more abundantly. When we clothe ourselves in righteousness, it does not mean that we have a self-righteous attitude, thinking that we are better than everyone else. It simply means that we wear virtue, worthiness, honesty, and decency.

> "The thief cometh not, but for to steal, and to kill, and to destroy: I am come that they might have life, and that they might have it more abundantly" (John 10:10 KJV).

When you feel discouraged, sad, angry, or even disappointed, remember that God has already united you with Jesus, who is wisdom. Jesus made things right for you. You don't have to go back to the old way, because there is a new way. When you clothe yourself in righteousness, you are saying, "I trust in God with my whole heart. Because of Jesus, there is nothing too big that it cannot be conquered – this was done for us before we were born. Yes, we have made mistakes, but because of Jesus, those mistakes will not tear us apart or keep our head hanging down. Yes, we have had many disappointments, but through Jesus we can live again in peace, success, and truth." So repenting of your sins, giving your life to Christ, and being born again is what is necessary to live a righteous life where you are in right standing with God. When you do this, you give God the go-ahead to make your life better. God honors us when we live righteously.

- "The mouth of the righteous is a fountain of life" (Proverbs 10:11 NIV).

When the righteous speaks, the speech restores. Here in Proverbs it is illustrated as a fountain. Just like a water fountain or a stream, it nourishes and gives life. Not only can humans drink from it, but also plants and animals can. So when you speak, remember that you are a fountain that brings life to everything around you.

- "The lips of the righteous feed many: but fools die for want of wisdom" (Proverbs 10:21 KJV).

Our words and actions can impact generations to come. There are many men and women who are great examples of godliness and leadership, they are creators that have left a legacy for us to follow. Their blueprint has been passed down and will continue through many generations. Still today, many around the world continue to celebrate and recognize heroic individuals and groups that have paved the way for us today. What we say and do can help each other. It can cause the tables to turn for the better. Then hope becomes visible and tangible. Wisdom brings change. As children of God, we should take care of each other in unity and peace.

- "No one can be established through wickedness, but the righteous cannot be uprooted" (Proverbs 12:3 NIV).

When we put our hope in Christ Jesus, the Bible says that we cannot be uprooted. This means that we are stable. This does not mean that we won't be faced with problems and tests, but it does mean that we have our faith and hope in the Almighty God. We know with assurance that no matter what comes our way, God will always provide and protect us.

- "Surely goodness and mercy shall follow me all the days of my life: and I will dwell in the house of the Lord forever" (Psalm 23:6 KJV).

When we live a righteous life, goodness and mercy will follow us. The Holy Spirit is our constant help and guide. It is beautiful to know that we can dwell in the house of the Lord forever. God will never leave us or forsake us.

- "When righteous men do rejoice, there is great glory: but when the wicked rise, a man is hidden" (Proverbs 28:12 KJV).

When the righteous person stands up, God's plan is revealed. There is great glory and victory that arises. Righteousness brings healing and restoration.

- "The Lord detests the way of the wicked, but he loves those who pursue righteousness" (Proverbs 15:9 NIV).

It pleases the Lord when we pursue righteousness. We were created for the purpose of building God's kingdom. This is a choice. Therefore, we should strive to be the very best example so that we can bring joy to ourselves, our families, and those who need to find their way.

9

DON'T MAKE EXCUSES; STAY ON COURSE

When I think about making an excuse, I associate it with time. Making excuse after excuse never gets you anywhere. Then, when you realize how much time has gone by with no results—it could be one year or even five years—you continue making the same excuses. Maybe your excuse is to blame someone else for your being where you are. Too many excuses can lead to deception in your mind, because then you begin to believe you have a valid reason for not looking for a better job, starting a business, eating healthier, hanging out with better friends, spending time with your family, etc. Making excuse after excuse can lead to poverty, missed opportunities, loss of focus, or involvement in things that you shouldn't do.

Our lives should be fruitful, not fruitless. We should be productive, using every ability and talent, fulfilling every idea, vision, and dream that God has given us. We should be lacking in nothing when it comes to our purpose. I, for one, have made many excuses, and when I looked back, I sensed that the time had gone by very fast. And then I thought, *Where would I have been if I would have stayed consistent?* When I could have been in a different place, a place of productivity, affluence, wealth, peace, and harmony, I was still in the beginning phase, still turning my wheels.

You will never reach your full potential if you continue to make excuses. Sometimes excuse are made when you don't think you're good enough or when you're scared of failure. Then you make up reasons in your mind for why things aren't accomplished, when you are the real reason why nothing is accomplished.

Don't settle for excuses. They are not an option. If you see it, you can accomplish it. When stumbling blocks are put in your way, figure out how to go around them, using Godly wisdom, love, and peace.

> "You did not choose me, but I chose you and appointed you so that you might go and bear fruit—fruit that will last—and so that whatever you ask in my name the Father will give you" (John 15:16 NIV).

When a new year approaches, we begin to set goals for ourselves. We prepare our minds for new challenges, and we look forward to what the new year will bring. We expect the new year to be better than former years. We want to gain everything we lost. We want to look better, feel better, and do better. But what if the unthinkable happens?

What if a month in, things don't go quite like you planned? What if your new routine starts to get boring or you don't see quick results? Or maybe you don't have the means to continue. Will you figure out a way to stay on course? The answer is yes, you will figure it out. You may not be able to reach your goal as quick as you thought, and you may have to make some changes, but do not take your eyes off your goal. It may take a little more time to get there, but enjoy the journey and learn from the process. Endurance develops our strength and character, according to Romans 5:4 (KJV).

STAYING FOCUSED

- When you seek God and his righteousness, all the things that you need and that you desire to have will be given to you (Matthew 6:33).

- Set your mind on good thoughts, not on what your facing (Colossians 3:2 KJV).

- God is our supplier. When you commit your plans, work, and ideas to the Lord, they will be supported and recognized (Proverbs 16:3).

- Have your eyes fixed on your goals. No matter what is around you—yes, you may have to deal with issues in the process—keep your gaze, as the Bible says, straight before you (Proverbs 4:25).

- Do not set your heart on things that will not make you a better person or cause you to go down the wrong path. When you make a mistake, learn from it. Be careful of these things. Guard your focus (Romans 5:8).

- Use what you have. When circumstances occur, they may slow you down a little, but use what you have and continue the journey. When you feel like you have no strength, use what you have. Use the little courage that you have even when you feel afraid. Find out what you do have that can be used when you run out of something. Use it until you can get what you would like to have. And, guess what? You're still on course; your eyes are still fixed on your goal. Second Kings 4 tells the story of the widow and the pots of oil. The widow had two sons and a pot of oil. She worried because she had nothing to pay off her husband's debt, and would have to satisfy the debt by giving up her sons. The prophet Elisha told the widow to pour the oil into jars. Once she did so, the oil began to multiply. She used what she had, along with her faith and action, even though it might have seemed impossible. She followed the instructions given by the prophet, and she and her sons were blessed. Not only did she have enough oil to pay off the debt, there was oil left over.

- Know your strength. Philippians 4:13 tells us that we can do all things through Christ who gives us strength. You are not weak but courageous. There is rest and peace when you get weary, and it is freely given to you. When Christ died for us, he overcame the world. God will give you peace in your heart. You can be joyful at all times if you choose to rest in him. God will give you peace in your mind, allowing you to sleep peacefully at night and walk daily in that same peace.

When you recognize a pattern of making excuses, stop for a moment and examine your thinking and your behavior. Give yourself a thorough evaluation. Asked God to help you in those areas of your life that need to be worked on. Pray continually for strength and endurance so that you are able to live a more productive life. Then you will be able to see the fruit of your labor and enjoy it, which will bring rest and peace, and love and harmony in the Holy Spirit. Finish your assignments and accomplish your plans; then you will be ready to move to greater levels. When you look back at where you started, you will see that your work was not hopeless. Be blessed!

LIVE YOUR DREAMS

The results of your life start with you as an individual, when you make up your mind to believe, behave, speak, and live with purpose. It starts at home, where parents teach their children right or wrong, love or hate, values or indecency. It starts from your upbringing, the hand you were dealt, your decisions, and how you see yourself. You are shaping not only your world but also the world of those around you, so set a solid foundation for yourself to enable you to live your dreams. A strong foundation is important for survival.

- the Word of God / Jesus Christ / biblical principles
- walking in love
- prayer / fasting
- having faith in God
- knowing who you are

It is not impossible for us to live our dreams. When we trust in God to see us through, even the tough times look easy.

Wherever you are in life, make up your mind to do the right thing and make the right choices by using wisdom. Evaluate yourself. If you have a problem with pride, selfishness, or greed, get rid of it. Anything that's holding you back from living your dreams to the fullest, ask God for help and guidance. Whether you're married or single, it starts with a vision. Perhaps you dream of graduating college, or having a successful marriage, prosperous business, successful children who are God fearing, good health, healthy relationships, or wealth. Whatever God has put inside you, don't deviate from it.

10

TAKE CARE OF YOURSELF
IN THE PROCESS

Come to Me, all of you who work and have heavy loads.
I will give you rest. Follow My teachings and learn from
Me. I am gentle and do not have pride. You will have rest
for your souls. For My way of carrying a load is easy and
my load is not heavy. (Matthew 11:28–30 NLT)

With everything that is going on around us, we can easily get distracted
if we are not careful.

Be mindful, not to lose yourself in the day-to-day, stay focused. When
conditions are thrown your way, if you don't watch with understanding,
you could neglect your family, waste time, and compromise the reason
for your existence.

"Devote yourselves to prayer with an alert mind and a
thankful heart" (Colossians 4:2 NLT).

A huge weight on the mind and body is having no peace. God
wants us to rest. He wants us to have his peace that is freely given to
us if only we will receive it. Colossians 3:15 tells us to let the peace
of God rule in our hearts. It also says that we are called to peace and
tells us to be thankful. First Peter 3:11 says that we must turn away

from evil, do good, and seek and pursue peace. Without peace, the physical body and mind is disrupted; it is not in a state of rest. We have to make the necessary changes to get the peace that God has already given to us. It's ours. Pursue peace; go after it. When you have peace, the right decisions are made and there is a better outcome. You are then able to hold on to it, walk in it, and share it.

Learn to quiet yourself. Get rid of the noise and hear the voice of God. Get the direction you need so that you can enter into his rest. Take a little time for yourself and fill your tank, get recharged. Get fueled up by feeding your spirit. When a person is hungry, it is hard for them to focus, but once they get some nourishment, the body begins to stabilize and is ready for work again. This is the same for our spirit. When it is not fed daily with the Word, its nourishment, it makes the body go off balance and become less stable.

STRESS LESS

Stress can be a major problem in your life if you allow it to be. Learning how to cope with stress is important if you want to live a successful life. It's easy to get stressed; just by thinking of all that's required in a day, seeing bills piled up on the table, hearing your car make an unusual sound, or just dealing with people day-to-day.

Stress can cause illness in the body, family problems, broken relationships, depression, weight loss or gain, unclear thinking, and even death, just to name a few. We cannot live effective lives if stress has taken over. So what do you do? Give all of your cares to God. Get rid of the clutter.

"Casting all your care upon him; for he careth for you" (1 Peter 5:7–9 KJV).

We should not be concerned about what tomorrow will bring, because tomorrow will take care of its self. I had to discipline myself when I would be worried or anxious. When negative thoughts would show up, I had to see a better outcome. I did this by training the way I view stressful situations. When a negative thought would present itself,

I would override that thought with a positive thought. I would say what God says about my life. I had to train myself so that worry and doubt would not over take me. I had to be careful not to add other people's problems to my life-along with all that was going on around me. If you are not careful you could be taking on personal problems and other people's problems at the same time; which would put a lot of pressure and stress on you.

Have you ever had someone dump their problems on you? Have you ever had someone rely on you to do everything for them because they did not want the responsibility and they gave it to you? I have learned to let go of what pulls me down and does not contribute to my success; and that it is okay to say no sometimes, do my part - and eliminate the extra stress. Now, I don't mean to let go of your family, your loved ones-not that kind of stress, although you have to establish balance and harmony in your home. I'm talking about the things that add no value to your life, like picking up a newspaper every morning for someone who can get his or her own, or rushing out earlier for work and neglecting your family, or maybe taking on too much work and become so busy that you lose yourself in the process. Maybe it's too much partying, spending too much money so you can keep up with friends and the latest trends, fear, afraid of failure, or just trying to please others. Stop stressing over worthless issues. Eliminate stress altogether. Remember—God will provide for you. He is your keeper. God knows what you need before you ask. And he will supply all that you need.

> "For your Father knoweth what things ye have need of, before ye ask him" (Matthew 6:8 KJV).

> "But my God shall supply all your need according to his riches in glory by Christ Jesus" (Philippians 4:19 KJV).

Don't let the cares of life rob you of your future. Your future and your family's future is more important than little issues you face. Stress can have a traumatic effect on your kids and your spouse; stress can tear a family apart. Don't let the enemy steal your joy and take you to a place where you are being unfruitful. The joy of the Lord is your strength.

When you start to feel sad or you sense depression or stress, say the following out loud (repeat it as many times as you need to): "The joy of the Lord is my strength." Add other scriptural verses to it if you need to. Speak the Word of God over your situation. Do not keep your mouth shut! God does not want us to lose our joy, but rather be confident in his love for us no matter what we face. He wants us to be consistent in our faith and not waver. Live blessed, not stressed!

FORGIVE AND FORGET

How many times have you said "I'll forgive, but I won't forget"? Have you asked yourself, "Was it something that I did to cause that person to offend or hurt me? Did I offend that person first?" Maybe such is not the case. It could be that you didn't do anything at all and that person lashed out at you and caused harm to you. Forgiveness is a tough area to deal with. All of us have been hurt numerous times by many people for various reasons, from our younger days to adulthood. The Bible speaks about forgiving those who have hurt or caused offense to us.

We should always evaluate ourselves, to see if we are wrong in a situation before we put the blame on someone else. Perhaps you were blameless and someone caused harmed to you or your family for no apparent reason, either through words, abuse, backbiting, not keeping their word, or being untrustworthy.

> Just a Thought
> Have you truly forgiven if you are unable to forget?

Here's what God's Word says:

- "I, even I, am he that blotteth out thy transgressions for mine own sake, and will not remember thy sins" (Isaiah 43:25 KJV).
- "For I will be merciful to their unrighteousness, and their sins and their iniquities will I remember no more" (Hebrews 8:12 KJV).

I have to say, there were times when I felt I was mistreated either by hurtful words, face-to-face, gossip, slander, wrong motives, and dishonesty on numerous occasions, and even though I said I forgave them, those thoughts would creep back in my mind.

Maybe your issue is not with others around you. You could be upset with yourself for making wrong decisions, or perhaps you are angry with God because your life isn't going as you had planned.

If you say you forgive others and yourself, why are you still holding on to the thoughts that make you bitter? Why aren't you speaking to the people who harmed you when you see them? Why aren't you praying for them if they treated you unfairly? Why can't you respectfully tell a person if he or she offended you and that you forgive them and move on? Why are you thinking less of yourself than you should? Why are you still angry with God? These are all questions that you should ask yourself when dealing with hurt. And when you deal with hurt that is close to home, this can really cause havoc. Unforgiveness is toxic to your physical body. It will break the body down to nothing. Do not hold hate and anger in your heart. When someone tries to mistreat us, use us, hurt us, or come against our children, it is our right to take a stand. But when we take a stand, God expects us to do it his way, not ours. For every situation, God will tell you just what to do and how to do it.

> "Be angry [at sin—at immorality, at injustice, at ungodly behavior], yet do not sin; do not let your anger [cause you shame, nor allow it to] last until the sun goes down" (Ephesians 4:26 AB).

> "Be not quick in your spirit to become angry, for anger lodges in the bosom of fools" (Ecclesiastes 7:9).

It might be hard sometimes when you want to take matters into your own hands, but God will fight for you.

> "Do not take revenge, my dear friends, but leave room for God's wrath, for it is written: 'It is mine to avenge; I will repay,' says the Lord" (Romans 12:19 NIV).

We should renew our minds daily. We may think that we are doing just fine and that we have no imperfections, but God knows our hearts. At one time, I thought I was consistent, had patience, and loved my enemies, but I was not as strong in those areas as I thought I was. It was a new season with new challenges. God has taught me that I have to be able to face every obstacle with consistency, bearing all fruits of the Spirit in every situation, not missing a beat. And I can accomplish this with his help. How would you feel if God were to remember all your sins and never forgive you for your mistakes? Would you say it's fair for God to act in such a way? So why do we act in such a way and simultaneously proclaim Jesus? After all, we are supposed to live our lives like Christ.

So we have to renew our minds daily. And always remember that it's not the person. The devil uses people and situations to agitate you, to get you off track, to bug you, and to hinder you. When I began to look at my life and what God has promised me, I discovered that it is far greater than holding grudges and having unforgiveness in my heart. And though it may take me a moment to get over the hurt or anger, nothing is too hard that is cannot be accomplished.

One day I went to the park because I needed a break and just wanted to clear my mind. I walked and talked with God, and I expressed how I felt about what people do and say. How can people be so selfish, saying they love while being discourteous? When will we learn and work together in unity and love, and stop the division and hate? My list went on as I talked to God.

Then I heard the Holy Spirit say, "Do what's right with what I give you. When I tell you to give, you give. When I tell you to move, you move." So in all of my complaining, God was working it out. I had to be careful not to get consumed with what was going on around me, as that would cause frustration, anger, and hopelessness.

So again, hold on to what you see for your life and do not accept anything less. Doors will open for you, at the appointed time if you stay on course.

REFLECTION

Is there unforgiveness in my heart toward someone? Are hurtful words or situations constantly playing in my mind? Do I talk about or ponder past events with anger or regret?

You have to be able to see when something comes to move you out of your peace, and you have to be able to cast down those thoughts and circumstances by rebuking them and thinking on a better ending. Change those thoughts and turn your situation around. What does God say about it?

11

YOU ARE CLOSER THAN YOU THINK

The LORD is my strength and my shield; my heart trusts
in him, and he helps me. My heart leaps for joy, and with
my song I praise him. (Psalms 28:7 NIV)

Things are not always what they seem. Like when you think someone
is a snob and that person is not that way at all; all because of what
someone told you. Or you are at a restaurant and it seems your server has
a bad attitude, only to find out that they are not feeling well. All of what is
seen on the outside is sometimes not that way at all. Occasionally Images
come to mind; people are placed in front of you with problems, mishaps,
and dysfunctions, all to get you bent out of shape and remove your peace.
We see examples almost daily of bad choices made by others or even
ourselves. When we make mistakes, we must learn from them, move on
and never make those choices again. What works for someone else may
not be the road that's best for you. What happens to another is not always
your end-result. We should stay away from evil and all things that will
cause us harm and has no benefit to our life. But, what God has revealed
to us, we should go after, trusting God and never compromise what we
see, because of another person. You should continue to stand firm on
God's Word because you are closer than you think to your victory.

Closer to what? Closer to knowing your purpose; closer to reaching
your goals; closer to your healing; closer to your breakthrough; closer to

a better you. It took me a long time to understand how to embrace my struggles and my pain. Life is not always easy, but it is not hard either. We don't always hit a home run, sometimes we get a curve ball and we miss it, sometimes we get a strike. But at the end, we win. Victory and success are in our DNA. We are created in God's image. Whatever He say's about us, is the truth of any matter. The Bible gives us direction and answers to everything. When challenges arise, embrace it. You're able to win any challenge. Rest in God, knowing that you can do all things through Christ. You can make anything happen with God.

That is why we labor and strive because we have put our hope in the living God, who is the Savior of all people, and especially of those who believe. 1 Timothy 4:10 (NIV)

You are closer than you think! Be fearless, not fearful; God has not given us a spirit of fear, but of power, love and a sound mind. We should be worry free and stress-free. Don't be ashamed of where you've been, you are renewed and a new creation in Christ, old things are passed away and all things are new according to 2 Cor 5:17.

Don't bring your past into your future. The resurrection of Christ replaced our past. We look forward to the end or the finishing of what we've started. How it will turn out; a new beginning. Our past brings us to our future, but our future should not bring us back to our past. In our past, we've suffered, endured, had joy and hope, abundance and peace. If you look back, I'm sure you will see where you've experienced if not all, a majority of these mentioned. The not so good was for a purpose even though it didn't always feel or seem that way, but that storm has ended. Let God continue to press you and push you to your next level. Don't give the devil credit for anything that God is doing. When you have fruit such as an orange or grape, you squeeze the fruit to get the goodness out of it; you are extracting out of that fruit what it was grown and purposed for. Like you and I, God squeeze and press us, just like we do when we eat fruit, we are pressed and squeezed to produce out of us what we were created for. Uncomfortable, yes – we may not want to keep our mouth shut but we have too; may not want to apologize but we must; may not want to be patient, but we must; may not want to go without, but we must. The pressing is uncomfortable, but it is satisfying in the end. We must be pushed sometimes, this is when our character is built, and our faith is stretched a little further than what we are used to, so that we can move to the next stages. Do you want better? Are you ready to go to the next level in your life? Are you tired of the same results? If you answered yes to any of these questions, then allow yourself to be pressed so that you can mature, be better, think differently, see differently and be victorious. If you feel that you have done all the things that you wanted and have accomplished more that you can ever imagine... guess what? There's greater in store for you. This is what makes God so awesome because even if you are 100 years of age there is still more to see, more to learn and more to do. This is that glorious life that we should all strive to experience. The joy and peace we've experienced is a constant reminder that we can have that same joy and peace every day of our lives. If God did it once he will do it again, his love, peace, and joy is always available to us - utilize what is freely given to you. Going back to dead works, actions that cause you grief is no longer an option. Ephesians 6:12, for we do not wrestle against flesh and blood, but against principalities, against powers, against the rulers of the darkness of this age, against spiritual hosts of wickedness in the heavenly places. Lean not to your own understanding but look to Christ for every need you have. If you see it, you can obtain it. It's not a thought that's impossible. You are closer than you think!

12

HAVE A WINNING ATTITUDE:
YOUR ATTITUDE MAKES A DIFFERENCE

> Therefore, since we are surrounded by such a huge crowd of witnesses to the life of faith, let us strip off every weight that slows us down, especially the sin that so easily trips us up. And let us run with endurance the race God has set before us. (Hebrews 12:1 NLT)

Since we are on a journey, there are challenges that we will face. Sometimes we don't ask for what is being handed to us, and we don't always understand it, but God has called us to endure the race that is set before us. And we have to do it with love, dignity, and character. Just as an athlete runs to win the gold medal, we, as children of God, are runners for Christ, trailblazers who continue to press toward the mark of the high calling that is in Christ Jesus. Though it may not always be easy, our race is to glorify God. In order to compete and win, we have to be fit for the race. Our attitude will determine our results. We are accountable for our actions, even through adversity. Having a positive attitude, even when it looks to be impossible, is key to finishing first. What others view as first place is not always what God sees as first place, because God looks at the heart, whereas people around us tend to look at the outer appearance.

You are called victorious, so there is no race that is too hard for you to win. Defeat is never an option for a winner. How you see yourself determines how you are going to finish. You should see yourself as a champion. I read an article once called the *7 Traits of Mentally Tough Runners*, written by JoAnn Dahlkoetter, PhD (www.competitor.com). This title captured my attention because it reminded me of what God's Word says about our lives and how we should live as we run the race that is set before us. The seven traits in the article are resilience, the ability to bounce back from adversity; focus, the ability to focus in the face of distractions or unexpected circumstances; strength, the ability to handle an unforeseen turn of events and remain balanced; preparation, the ability to anticipate situations ahead of time and feel prepared; vision, the ability to keep moving forward with our objective; openness, the ability to learn and be open to all possibilities; and trust, the ability to believe in ourselves.

In comparison, from a biblical standpoint, I was amazed at how closely related the seven traits are to our daily living. Let's take a look.

- Resilience – Corinthians 4:8–9 (NIV)
  "We are hard pressed on every side, but not crushed; perplexed, but not in despair; persecuted, but not abandoned; struck down, but not destroyed."

- Focus – Proverbs 4:25–27 (MSG)
  "Keep your eyes straight ahead; ignore all sideshow distractions. Watch your step, and the road will stretch out smooth before you. Look neither right nor left; leave evil in the dust."

- Strength – Isaiah 40:31 (NLT)
  "But those who trust in the Lord will find new strength. They will soar high on wings like eagles. They will run and not grow weary. They will walk and not faint."

- Preparation – 1 Thessalonians 5:6 (AB)
  "So then let us not sleep [in spiritual indifference] as the rest [of the world does], but let us keep wide awake [alert and cautious] and let us be sober [self-controlled, calm, and wise]."

- Vision – Habakkuk 2:3 (NLT)
  "This vision is for a future time. It describes the end, and it will be fulfilled. If it seems slow in coming, wait patiently, for it will surely take place. It will not be delayed."

- Openness – 2 Timothy 3:16–17 (NIV)
  "All Scripture is God-breathed and is useful for teaching, rebuking, correcting and training in righteousness, so that the servant of God may be thoroughly equipped for every good work."

- Trust – Proverbs 3:5–6 (NLT)
  "Trust in the Lord with all your heart; do not depend on your own understanding. Seek his will in all you do, and he will show you which path to take."

It may take months or even years to reach your goal, but stay focused. Keep your mind on the end, on what you want to accomplish, and see yourself winning. If you've decided to lose a few pounds by eating healthy and exercising regularly but you get on the scale and see you've gained instead, stay focused. If you've decided to save $100 per month and there is an unexpected bill that sets you back about four months, continue saving, keeping your mind on your goal. When your five-year plan turns into an eight-year plan, don't get frustrated; keep going. Don't stop applying for jobs just because you were turned down many times before; keep applying. Your attitude will determine if you win or lose, and it will set the tone for your day. Your attitude will determine your outcome.

During the last months of completing Keys and a Mirror, I wondered if I would ever complete what I started. I had to push my way through it all. I encouraged myself, read scriptures and declarations, listened to several teachings, reshaped my attitude whenever necessary, and identified when I was getting off course. I created a visual picture of myself accomplishing everything I had started and much more. Others were there to encourage me when worry and doubt tried to sit in. I was reminded that each day would take care of its self each time God provided for me, and that I should be optimistic and focus on winning. Satan wants to destroy us. If we allow the devil to take our joy, he will shatter our dreams.

"The tongue has the power of life and death, and those who love it will eat its fruit" (Proverbs 18:21 NIV).

- A soft answer (Proverbs 15:1). The way you address someone or the tone in which you answer is a reflection of you. You are the best example for someone else.
- A teachable heart. I believe that one of the greatest down falls is when we think that we know it all, are always right and have all the answers. When we don't allow ourselves to be teachable, we limit our ability to do greater.
- Your attitude will make a difference. A good attitude brings hope and substance to any circumstance. Even if it doesn't help the next person, it is good for your well-being.
- Your countenance matters. Your facial expression can sometimes tell the story. It not only makes you feel unmotivated but also affects the people around you. Be joyful, even when you don't feel like it, it will make you feel so much better. By keeping your joy in the midst of all adversity, even when you don't feel like it, will not only build your character but also give you peace and victory.

RESPECT AND GRATITUDE

To win the race, we must value each other, we must respect each other and show gratitude. When you are on your road to success, there are people around you that can help get you to the finish line, even down to the youngest child. Just like the runner, there are people along the way that gives the runner water, towels, encouragement to finish the race, first aid, there's someone to remind the runner of the amount of time and laps that are left in the race. It takes a team effort. Just because you are the runner and the trophy will be yours when you win, does not mean that you did it all yourself. Yes, you've trained hard and have put countless hours in, but others were needed along the way in some shape or form. It's a collaborative effort. Do not devalue another's contribution or viewpoint - because all is needed for your success. Show gratitude for those around you that contributes to your vision, down to the least amount of involvement. If others are kind enough to help you, be gracious enough to acknowledge those that put in their time and effort. Be kind, be grateful, and never boast in what you can do or what you have – it's a collaborative effort. Be humble, be strong, and be unified. Share your reward in the end with greater purpose, understanding and value.

HOW TO WIN:

- Fast and pray
- Ask God for direction.
- Stay focused.
- Don't let others detour you.
- Be positive at all times.
- Affirm yourself daily by seeing yourself the way God sees you.
- Know that even though you may lose sometimes, you are still a winner.
- Be respectful and show gratitude
- Know who you are in Christ and know your purpose.

<u>Bonus</u>

The year 2020 has changed our world drastically. From a Pandemic, to the loss of love ones, social distancing, racial violence, the fight for equality, unemployment, panic, and stress. The entire world is affected by the up-stir. In these times, we cannot put our faith in people or even ourselves. Put your faith in the living God, trust him. He is the only one who can heal your hurt, take away your pain, and position you to prosper in perilous times. God is the only one who can keep you safe, free your mind, elevate you even when others say there is no hope. You can have hope and assurance during a time of drought. The blood of Jesus covers us. God's spirit lives inside of us. We are mighty in battle through God. He will never leave us or forsake us. God will raise you to a level of Purpose, Position, Power and Prosperity. God's grace and favor will follow you because you have put all your trust in him.

I am sure most would agree that we have had a considerable amount of time to reflect during the past few months. And if you have not, I encourage you to take some time to do so. Look at your life, look in the mirror and take your position, pick up the keys that you have been given. We were created for a purpose and it is our obligation to find out what it is, so that others can be blessed through our life. We are not trash nor rubbish, we are kings and priest that are to reign in the earth, without limitations, through holiness, and by walking in the fruit of the Spirit. (Galatians 5:22-23)

Unity Power Change

When we are *Unified*, we gain *Power* which leads to *Change*. We gain progress which causes us to prosper and be successful. When Unity is in operation, change will take place. It puts us in a position to carry out our God-given assignments.

How can we become unified with so much division in the world? Not everyone will agree with you on a new perspective on life. So be ready for a few hurtles but just know that there are others that will agree and cheer you own. Don't wait for others to make the first step, you be the first to make it. And when you take the 1st step, make it count – people are depending on you. Don't wait for someone else to set the trend, you be the 1st to do it. There are many who are waiting on your gift, your knowledge and wisdom. There are people that share the same goals as you, who are working on similar projects, and they are waiting for you to arrive.

I encourage you to use your authority and power to change the world for the better.

Not in the eyes of men, but in the eyes of God. (Proverbs 3:7)
Kevin Stewart, Jr.
14 yrs old

Trust, believe and follow the Lord!
Jaleel Stewart
8 yrs old

Printed in the United States
By Bookmasters